"Stephen Miller's new book offers us the fruit of his many years of serving as worship leader and lover of the gospel. Thankfully, Worship Leaders, We Are Not Rock Stars does not read like a book written by an expert with a chip on his shoulder, rather by a called man with a burden on his heart—a man who has obviously been humbled and gladdened by the God of all grace. With the wisdom than can only come with years and tears, and with practical insights of a seasoned veteran, Stephen's book offers timely advice and rich encouragement to worship leaders and congregants alike."

— **Scotty Smith**, founding pastor of Christ Community Church,
author of *The Reign of Grace* and *Restoring Broken Things*

"Worship Leaders, We Are Not Rock Stars is much needed and long overdue. It is directed to those who lead us in cooperate worship as we honor King Jesus when we sing, but it is also a book pastors would do well to heed! In these pages you will find words of wisdom that are honest and insightful. Hidden sins of the heart are exposed and biblical solutions are provided. I love Stephen's heart and his transparency. I also love the vision he cast for those who occupy what is nothing less than an office of the church. There is no place in the church for rock stars or superstars. There is only a place for a Savior whose name is Jesus. Stephen Miller makes this clear. Thank you, my brother."

— **Daniel L. Akin**, president of South Eastern Baptist Theological Seminary

"With warmth and vulnerability, Stephen Miller invites us on a journey to recover the vocation of 'worship leader.' He explores the key dimensions of this role, with a careful examination of Scripture on every page. If a new generation of worship leaders would read and discuss this book, our churches would be better for it. After all, what we do when we gather in worship as the people of God becomes what we believe, for better or for worse. Worship doesn't just reflect our faith; it forms it. This book will help our worship leaders form our faith in richer ways."

— **Glenn Packiam**, pastor of New Life Downtown, author of
Discover the Mystery of Faith: How Worship Shapes Believing

"Stephen Miller is right. Jesus builds his church on a Rock (Matthew 16:18), but not on rock stars. In this book you will find bold, convictional, practical wisdom on leading worship that is neither boring nor entertainment-based. We can all use this sort of reframing of the most important thing we do in this age or in the age to come."

> — **Russell D. Moore**, president, Ethics & Religious Liberty Commission, Southern Baptist Convention

"I've always known Stephen Miller to be a man of passion and integrity whether in writing music, leading worship, or leading his family. The principles that guide him as a worshiper both on and off the stage shine through in Worship Leaders, We Are Not Rock Stars."

> — **Matt Carter**, pastor of The Austin Stone, coauthor of *For The City* and *The Big Win*

"Jesus is our ultimate worship leader, and He didn't come as an entertainer, but as a servant. As such, worship leaders should see themselves first and foremost as 'worship servants' who point worshipers to Christ, not to themselves. Whatever the style of worship in our churches and however old our songs, the temptation to entertain is real. This book calls pastors, elders, deacons, musicians, and all those leading in worship to strive to get our eyes off ourselves so that worshipers will be less distracted by us and, thus more focused on worshiping God according to His Word."

> — **Burk Parsons**, copastor of Saint Andrew's Chapel, Editor of *Tabletalk*

"Worship Leaders, We are Not Rock Stars is a helpful contribution in the conversation of what worship leaders are, and what they are not. Elevating the role of the worship leader leads to gross idolatry. Diminishing the role of the worship leader departs from biblical church leadership. I pray that this book helps clarify the role of worship leaders as we set out to serve our local congregations in gospel ministry."

> — **Matt Boswell**, pastor of ministries and worship at Providence Church, Frisco, TX, founder of Doxology & Theology

WORSHIP LEADERS
WE ARE NOT ROCK STARS

STEPHEN MILLER

MOODY PUBLISHERS
CHICAGO

Scripture quotations are taken from *The Holy Bible, English Standard Version*. Copyright © 2000; 2001 by Crossway Bibles, a division of Good News Publishers. Used by permission. All rights reserved.

Edited by Jim Vincent
Cover and interior design: Design Corps
Author Photo: Will Cobert

Library of Congress Cataloging-in-Publication Data

Miller, Stephen, 1983-
 Worship leaders, we are not rock stars / Stephen Miller.
    pages cm
Includes bibliographical references.
ISBN 978-0-8024-0986-7
1. Public worship. 2. Christian leadership. I. Title.
BV25.M66 2013
264'.2--dc23

                                          2013012818

We hope you enjoy this book from Moody Publishers. Our goal is to provide high-quality, thought-provoking books and products that connect truth to your real needs and challenges. For more information on other books and products written and produced from a biblical perspective, go to www.moodypublishers.com or write to:

Moody Publishers
820 N. LaSalle Boulevard
Chicago, IL 60610

1 3 5 7 9 10 8 6 4 2

Printed in the United States of America

CONTENTS

FOREWORD

The relationship between a pastor and a worship leader is usually tenuous at best. You would think the relationship would be easy. After all, both the worship leader and lead pastor have the same goal: To help people see Jesus and respond in worship. They both have the same currency: words that are used to describe God and inspire others to obedience.

Though our goals are similar, our arguments are frequent. The arguments I have with our worship leaders are numerous. We argue about song selections. Should we do more hymns or fewer? We argue about length of service. I always think it isn't a big deal to cut a song or two, and the worship leader shockingly questions the wisdom of an hour-long sermon. Most of these arguments end with me reminding our said leader that Satan originally had the title of worship leader.

The reality is that pastors and worship leaders really are on the same team, and we are fighting the same battles. Together we fight the consumerism that congregants bring from their lives into the corporate gathering, demanding that both worship and preaching meet every felt need in their lives without causing them too much trouble. Together we fight the ever-evolving but never-dispassionate "worship wars" among God's people with regard to song and style preferences. Together we fight apathy in faithful saints who are worn down from a week of battling the world, the flesh, and the devil. In like manner, pastor and worship leader struggle with pride, selfish ambition, and rock stardom every time we lead out with our gifts.

As a pastor I need resources that help me understand the artists who lead God's people to the throne in gathered worship. I need to understand how to make song and sermon most glorifying and most edifying. I need to learn how to journey with my worship leader into the path of dying to self so that Christ may truly come alive in us as we lead on Sunday. *Worship Leaders, We Are Not Rock Stars* is a godsend.

Whether you are a seasoned pastor or a newbie in leading God's people, this book will help you with the practical challenges of everyday ministry. It is hard for me to choose whether this book helps pastors or worship leaders more. No choice is needed. Take the time to read and heed, so that all of us who minister God's name can make Jesus famous.

DARRIN PATRICK

Lead Pastor of The Journey, St. Louis, MO, and author of *For the City; Church Planter: The Man, the Message, the Mission;* and *A Dude's Guide to Manhood: Finding True Manliness in a World of Counterfeits.*

FREE
DOWNLOAD

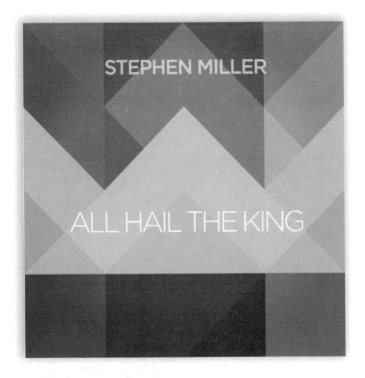

STEPHEN MILLER

ALL HAIL THE KING

WORSHIP LEADERS

ROCK STAR WORSHIP
SYNDROME

It's such a vivid memory . . . the first time I experienced a real rock band leading worship. Full drum kit, electric guitars, bass, and four keyboards—five dudes decked out in the finest apparel Gadzooks and Hot Topic had to offer in the mid-1990s.

The lead singer, a guy with a shaved head and larger-than-life goatee, wore a silver sequin button-up and jumped around a lot while slapping his leather-pant-clad thigh.

The bass player wore a sleeveless black shirt with stainless-steel studs adorning his "I work out more than you" shoulders. Standing at least a good six feet five inches, he was the ladies' favorite by far.

The electric guitar player stood a good bit shorter, but he looked like the kind of bad boy that every girl wants to try to make good. Spiky, jet-black hair, hemp necklace, eleven bracelets on each wrist, a ring on every finger, and form-fitting, distressed dark jeans.

Together they looked just like a group on MTV, which still played music videos back then. I had never seen anything like it in corporate worship before and I was immediately taken up with it.

I grew up in a family that moved around every couple of years, and in each small Oklahoma or Texas town we went to, we immediately found the First Baptist Church of Fill-in-the-Blank-Town. That church was our home for the duration of our stay.

I don't think "worship leader" was even a category back then. The approved titles were "music minister" or "choir and orchestra director" or whatever the church thought was fitting for the man whose job description was to wear a three-piece suit, comb his hair in a Reaganesque style, plan an annual Mega Christmas Extravaganza Pageant event, and choose from a preset, congregation-approved list of fifty hymns and fifteen choruses to lead the music portion of the service. The perfect combination of these factors was sure to adequately prepare the congregation for the truly important part of the service: the pastor's message.

I had affectionately named this 1980s forerunner of the worship leader "Hand Wavey Guy." I mean no disrespect with this title, but as a kid, I simply called them like I saw them. When I say "Hand Wavey Guy," you know exactly who I am referring to. You probably had him waving those hands at you when you were growing up too—back and forth, up and down to the beat, over and over.

But more than leading us in worship of our almighty Creator and King, it felt to me like Hand Wavey Guy was leading us in a series of boring calisthenic rudiments: stand up, sit down, stand up, sit down, rinse, repeat, and then in the words of Brian McKnight, "If ever I believe my work is done, then start it back at one."

Worship services were cold at worst and cheesy at best. There was hardly anything a kid would connect with, and it was hard to believe anyone else could. Honestly, who wouldn't love epic timpani-driven renditions of "Saved! Saved! Saved!" and high-energy choral arrangements of songs about diadems and whatnot? When churches finally started to try to address the situation, ruthless worship wars broke out between the hymn lovers and the chorus lovers. In most cases, they came to a stalemate because the hymn lovers gave the most money. And thus "blended worship" was invented.

The product of blended worship was an even lamer version of cheeseball quirkiness than before, and now no one was happy. I still recall Hand Wavey Guy at a particular church in Texas really trying to get edgy and relevant, so he created a mash-up where "I'll Fly Away" got down with Lenny Kravitz's hit song "Fly Away" and made a gloriously tacky song child. Ladies and gents, that was about as good as it got.

As a result, while my mom made me go to church every time the doors were open (something for which I am exceedingly thankful now), I would have much rather stayed home and played *Super Mario Brothers* on my Nintendo or *Prince of Persia* on my computer. A few times, due to my Oscar-worthy performances, I was able to fake being sick well enough to stay home. I perceived this to be a great victory, flying in the face of the institution.

I suppose that the pendulum response to this era of uber-irrelevant, fake-a-sickness-to-avoid-it ministry was, over time, to make worship services look as little like that as possible.

And so there I stood in a "worship service" that was about as far away from what I grew up experiencing as you could get. At the time,

I loved it. I drank the rock star worship leader Kool-Aid and it tasted good! I wanted to be just like the rock stars who got to do music for Jesus. I actually bought the shiny shirts and hemp necklaces (though weighing something like three hundred pounds, I couldn't pull off the leather pants) and started leading worship in my youth group. For years I never even considered putting a hymn in my "set list" because they just weren't cool and you simply couldn't slap your knee and jump around as effectively to the Doxology. I didn't want to be Hand Wavey Guy . . . I wanted to be Rock Star Worship Leader Man.

Fast forward a few years: That rock star worship band that had once inspired me had broken up, in part because the lead singer came out as gay. Additionally many of their fans who had aspired to be just like them had completely dropped out of ministry or had never started at it to begin with. I too stopped leading worship for a couple of years in order to start a "band full of Christians"—but not a Christian band—and pursue a record deal.

At the young age of twenty-one, with patient kindness, God led me to repentance away from the pursuit of a life of rock stardom and called me back to this ministry of leading His people in worship through singing. I didn't want to be Hand Wavey Guy or Rock Star Worship Leader Man, but those seemed like my only two options. Wasn't there something between the extremes? It may have been out of pure arrogance or ignorance, but I set out to live in the in-between and be something different.

I wasn't the only one on this journey, as I soon found out. It seemed like every young worship leader I talked to was on the same quest, hoping for something relevant to their generation. Hoping to make some sort of musical art for the church that was fulfilling for them personally and not

> I wanted to be just like the rock stars who got to do music for Jesus.

embarrassing for their friends to see them doing.

It's amazing how much change can happen in a decade. There are now more styles of worship under the sun than I would have ever imagined when I first surrendered my life to ministry. We are no longer confined to any specific musical style or worship style or service style. Churches have multiple venues, and each venue has a different musical flavor. Yet with the advent of the modern worship movement, I have come to realize that the rock star worship syndrome I experienced early on is not so much a musical style or way of dressing, but is an attitude and mentality that hides itself in various ways, some more obvious than others. And Hand Wavey Guy is just as susceptible to it as any acoustic-guitar-wearing pop-music lover, singing the latest, hippest worship song. How did we get here?

Walk into your average Christian conference or megachurch on a given weekend and what do you see? Most often, a supercool worship leader wearing skinny jeans, a fedora, and a scarf (though it's 90 degrees outside) with a tattoo on whichever forearm he raises in worship, standing on a massive stage with an incredible light show and people screaming out in worshipful adoration. It sounds, and looks, a lot like a rock concert.

I am not saying that you can't love Jesus and have a savvy fashion sense. They are not mutually exclusive. Though my frame isn't quite suited for skinny jeans, I do like a good scarf (in the winter) and a tattoo as much as any other guy. Some of the most God-loving, Christ-exalting, gospel-centered worship leaders I know dress better than Urban Outfitters cover models and have tattoos that would impress Kat Von D herself. They serve in large churches that have large stages and excellent lighting systems and they use all of those things as tools to exalt Christ.

I know many suit-wearing worship pastors who lead choirs and orchestras really well in an effort to connect with their context for the glory and worship of Jesus Christ. They can bring tears to people's eyes by singing better than Pavarotti and yet remain some of the most humble people on earth. I also know that there are many suit-wearing choir and orchestra worship pastors who are some of the biggest prima donnas a man could ever meet and are filled with high-church snobbery, pride over their GQ swag that makes elderly women swoon, and arrogance that their way is far superior to others'.

The problem is that for many, the tools of worship have become a substitute for actual worship of Christ. It's not necessarily their fault. It's a result of the emotionally driven celebrity culture we have created and modeled for them in the church. When a leader is talented and charismatic in personality, we tend to put them on the proverbial pedestal and blur the line between admiration and worship, between imitating them as they imitate Christ and substituting them for Christ. With music, this is all the more dangerous because we are dealing with a naturally emotional medium.

Emotions are not bad in and of themselves. They are quite useful in engaging us holistically in worship.

Consider how Jonathan Edwards, the great theologian and pastor, put it:

> I don't think ministers are to be blamed for raising the affections of their hearers too high, if that which they are affected with be only that which is worthy of affection, and their affections are not raised beyond the proportion to their importance, or worthiness of affection. I should think myself in the way of my duty to raise the affections of my hearers as high as possibly I can, provided that they are affected

> We tend to put a talented, charismatic leader on the proverbial pedestal and blur the line between admiration and worship.

*with nothing but truth, and with affections that are not
disagreeable to the nature of what they are affected with.[1]*

It is the job of worship leaders to raise the affections of the people we lead to the highest possible height with the truth of the worthiness of God in our songs. And yet, while emotions are helpful handmaids of worship, the emotional and even sensual nature of music can make it difficult to know whether we are raising the affection of our hearers with the truth or simply the thrill of the song. We may go for the emotional jugular and completely fail to exalt the character, holiness, and majesty of God. The music becomes self-serving.

Perhaps just as common and deadly of a practice, however, is to use even the deepest truths of God to serve our own prideful pursuit of platform and prominence. Because we are in a culture that makes "idols" out of men and women who can sing, people may have a difficult time not putting talented worship leaders in the rock-star limelight. This is a very tempting place to be as a worship leader, as that sort of public appreciation can be intoxicating. But fame and glory are well-trained assassins, and they have slain many who have pursued them for themselves.

If you think about it logically, the idea of Christian celebrity is laughable. Fame is a fickle friend who stays with you as long as you pay up, then bails when it loses interest.

I recently saw a list of the top 100 songs from the 1990s. As I asked my wife if she remembered any of the artists, she could only name around five of them. Back then, they were big deals with millions of dollars and hoards of fans! Yet now their

> Are we raising the affection of our hearers with the truth or simply the thrill of the song?

legacies live on only in a list.

As I write this, Justin Bieber is a teen music sensation who has 23 *million* followers on Twitter. Lady Gaga has 25 million. Katy Perry has 20 million. These are the top music celebrities of 2012. In contrast, the top Christian music celebrities have anywhere from 100,000 to 350,000 followers, which is roughly 1 percent of Justin or Katy. Where will they be in ten years? Only time will tell.

At some base level, we all know that fame is fleeting. That it will stab us in our backs when we aren't looking. That it only wants to take and never wants to give. But even if for a moment, it feels very good to be wanted, applauded, and loved.

You may be at a church of fifty or five thousand, worshiping to indie folk, pop rock, or simply organ and piano. You may be age twenty-five or you may be seventy-five. I don't know who you are as you read this, but it is highly likely that simply because of the culture we live in, you are currently or have struggled with rock star worship syndrome yourself. You are not alone. But you don't have to give in.

You have been called to something much greater. You have been redeemed by Jesus and adopted into His family, then called to lead His church. You have been given the gift of musical art to tell the gospel and connect people's hearts to their Savior. You have been made a teacher to mold people's thinking about who God is and what He has done.

Together, we can walk through who we have been called to be as worship leaders. But one thing is certain: we are not rock stars.

WORSHIP LEADERS

1

WHAT ARE
WE?

I have to be honest with you. This book is somewhat a reaction against what I have seen in the larger church culture of the world. The overwhelming misunderstanding of what a worship leader actually is and what the measure of success for a worship leader is has left me with a great measure of concern.

Even as I write this, I am dumbfounded, staring at an online ad that says, "Are you a worship leader? Click here to learn how to sign a record deal, get radio airplay, and start playing real paid gigs."

To be totally candid, I had three immediate reactions:

→ Anger

→ Grief

→ A little bit of throw-up in my mouth

At what point did the measure of success in ministry become record deals, radio play, and real gigs? Yet this is the definition of worship leading for much of the world. This has become the pursuit and the end goal.

Don't get me wrong; these are not bad things in and of themselves. If you are writing songs and producing quality art that a record label can come alongside to help take those songs to the larger church for the edification and encouragement of the masses, then by all means, go for it!

If you have a good song that I can hear on the radio instead of some musically mediocre theological train wreck of a song, then I am all for that.

If you are called to full-time vocational ministry, and you can provide for your family by leading the church in worship with excellence, you should be paid for your labor.

But the simple fact remains that most worship leaders will never have these things. For most, this is a completely unrealistic expectation or goal to have, and the overemphasis of these things as the measure of success has left scores of worship leaders feeling like broken failures.

Most worship leaders will plod away as bivocational ministers, never to be celebrated by anyone other than their local congregation and God Himself.

And that is okay.

So when I see anything that holds up an unhealthy, unhelpful measure of a successful worship leader, I react.

But in my reaction I want to be careful not to swing the pendulum and focus entirely on all the things that are wrong with a situation, rather than pointing to ways to take positive strides forward. I have seen this focus on "here's what's wrong" happen over and over again; and while it's useful for building a following, it's less helpful in digging us out of the proverbial lurch.

I have heard sermon after sermon preached completely in the negative. "The gospel is not this and the gospel is not that. The gospel does not _____ and the gospel does not _____."

Many churches and ministries base their entire existence on what they are not. "We are not one of those churches that _____. When you come to our church, you're not gonna see _____."

The blogosphere is full of people who have made a name for themselves by ripping the many forms of the modern evangelical church to shreds.

For the first sixteen years of my life the only thing I heard about what it meant to be a Christian was, "Don't smoke, don't drink, don't chew, and don't date girls who do."

It is easier to criticize than to encourage.

So it would be really easy for me to write an entire book on all the things that a worship leader is not. But that wouldn't actually move us any closer to an understanding of what exactly a worship leader is.

I use the term "worship leader" very intentionally.

It is not in the Bible and I know that there are many other titles that I could use that would potentially be less controversial. For example: song leader, music director, or even choir master if we're going strictly biblical. After all, Jesus is our truest and ultimate worship leader—our High Priest

> The blogosphere is full of people who enjoy ripping the many forms of the modern evangelical church to shreds. It is easier to criticize than to encourage.

and Mediator who leads us to the throne of God (something a man could never do) and allows us to worship by the power of the Holy Spirit.

Directly underneath Jesus stands the lead pastor of the local church, who functionally acts as the primary worship leader. While he may not lead the church in congregational singing (though he very well may), he is an undershepherd of the Chief Shepherd, joining with Jesus in directing the worship of the sheep in his care through the preaching of the Word and much, much more.

So with those things in mind, I want to answer very intentionally what may be the first objection or question that arises; namely, "Why call ourselves "worship leaders"?"

Not only is "worship leader" an easily understood and widely identifiable title for the person who leads the church in corporate worship, but it is also perhaps the most helpful and descriptive because it refuses to limit the worship of God within the church to singing only. The Bible is clear that worship has an all-of-life-ness about it that can't be relegated to just singing.

While singing has a powerful and unique role in worship, songs may be our smallest expression of worship. To call a worship leader a worship leader is to say that his responsibilities go far beyond simply leading the church in singing some songs.

A worship leader is to be a person who exemplifies worship in all areas of life as an example for the church to emulate; who pursues God with everything and lives a life of holiness that worships through obedience in all things; who leads the church in an all-encompassing lifestyle of worship.

Part of the disconnect that has led to the prominence of rock star worship syndrome

> Worship has an all-of-life-ness about it that can't be relegated to just singing.

in the church is that people have failed to understand this all-of-life nature of worship. They want to compartmentalize worship to the seventy-five minutes on Sunday morning.

If Sunday morning songs are the church's only worship experience all week, there is no wonder that we have placed such a hard emphasis on having the best, most musically gifted song leader. But such a focus on music and the music leader is often at the detriment to the myriad other aspects of worship, both personal and corporate.

Songs are only a piece of corporate worship, but true worship leaders effectively use those songs in concert with a lifestyle of worship, as tools to accomplish Christ's pastoral purposes in the lives of the people they are leading.

So if a worship leader is not just a song leader or music director, then what is he or she? That's what I want to communicate with this book. In fact, at one point it was suggested that I not call this book "Worship Leaders, We're Not Rock Stars," but rather "What Is a Worship Leader?"

The latter just didn't quite have the same ring to it. In fact, it sounded quite boring to me, as I'm sure you'll agree, because you probably wouldn't be reading this book right now if I had called it something as boring as all that. Yet that is the very question I want to answer in the coming pages. If we're not rock stars—and we've pretty much agreed that's not us—then what are we?

In some way, I hope to equip you with a higher sense of calling and ambition for great, lasting impact gospel ministry to the church. I hope to instill a sense of the gravity of our responsibility and the greatness of our privilege.

Over the next few chapters, I will break down the role of worship leaders within the church—their identity, responsibilities,

> If we're not rock stars, then what are we?

privileges, and challenges. Just to give you a preview of where we are going, here are my points:

→ *We are the redeemed and adopted.* Until we know that our identity in Christ is far better than any identity that we could try to attain to through the applause of man, we will constantly be jockeying for positions of prominence. Our greatest identity is not in being a worship leader, how many songs we write, how big our church is, or even radio play. Our greatest identity is in being children of God who are created in His image, redeemed by His blood, indwelt by His Spirit, adopted into His family, given an eternal inheritance, sent out on His mission, while we are being sanctified and increasingly formed into His image as we prepare for our eternal home with Him. Everything else pales in comparison.

→ *We are worshipers.* This seems a bit like a no-brainer, but we are created to worship, and we are all always worshiping something or someone. Because of our fallen state, our hearts are prone to replace the perfect Giver with His good gifts—including the gifts of ministry, spiritual influence, and affirmation. These gifts are all good, but they are not the goal. Remember, true worshipers of God don't primarily worship Him publicly on stage or in the pews of churches. They pursue God in secret—in all of life for the holy goal of knowing Him, being known by Him, and making Him known.

→ *We are pastors and deacons.* We are not primarily musicians or song singers. God has given us the great privilege and responsibility of teaching, shepherding, and caring for His people. He has set the qualifications bar high for anyone who would serve His church in this way. These are not merely suggestions, but a standard set for us in the Bible, which He has given us that we might know Him and make Him known.

→ *We are theologians.* Worship leaders are teachers of doctrine in the worship service. Every song is teaching something to the people who are singing it, whether it is rich in doctrinal truth or riddled with heresy. It is the job of the worship leader to be diligent in guarding the doctrines that are taught in the songs he or she leads.

→ *We are storytellers* (*liturgists*). Worship leaders do not simply write out set lists. They should carefully and skillfully craft the order of worship to best shape the gospel for the people they are leading. We craft the liturgy, or order of the worship service, to tell the story in fresh, full ways each week. As liturgists, we consider how each element in the order of worship plays a vital part in doing that. From the call to worship, to adoration to confession and assurance, to songs of mission and sending, each portion of the service has a purpose that worship leaders should know and wield with efficiency and excellence to propel forward the wonderful story of God's greatness and our worth in Him alone.

→ *We are evangelists.* The role of the worship leader is, by nature, an evangelistic role. Each week, the content of our songs and the order in which we do them, as well as our prayers, Scripture readings, and more should be masterfully selected to present the gospel of Jesus Christ in a compelling way to those whom the Spirit is drawing. Additionally, as followers of Christ who have been filled with and empowered by the Spirit of God, we are to go outside the walls of the church and make loud the good news of who Christ is and what He has done.

→ *We are artists.* We are created in the image of the ultimate Artist to be artistic, as He is. Because of the nature of music in worship, there is a creativity that we must explore. However, while creativity is a wonderful servant to worship, it is a terrible master. Worship leaders ought to always diligently strive to maintain the tension of creative artistic expression and helpful practices for maximum corporate engagement.

→ *We are Christians.* The life of a worship leader is the life of a normal, average, run-of-the-mill Christian. We are not special and unique snowflakes. We are not exempt from living as disciples or making disciples. We are living sacrifices, whose lives should overflow with the fruit of righteousness that comes from walking in obedience by faith. Like all Christians, we should be consumed with an unceasing passion for the supremacy of the name and glory of Jesus Christ in all we say and do.

To help us better understand our various roles and ministries as leaders of worship, this chapter and others that follow will end with "Questions for Leaders." These questions are ideal for personal study or as a group activity—consider having your entire worship team meeting weekly to discuss and apply these concepts. It could change your group—and their worship.

As we explore our roles together in the coming pages, I pray that God will give both you and me an intense gratitude for His rescuing us from being dead in our sins and raising us to life for this work—a work that He had planned for us before He created the foundations of the world (Ephesians 1:3–5; 2:10). That He would give us a sober mind to not think too highly of our position or too lowly of our position, but to think rightly about our position and to rise to its demands with humble, gentle, and faithful servants' hearts. May nothing short of our faithfulness to the Spirit's work in and through us be the measure of our success. And may we be content with that.

QUESTIONS FOR LEADERS

1. What comes to mind when you think of what it means to be a worship leader?

2. What lies have you been believing about what success looks like for a worship leader?

3. What statement in this chapter surprised you? Why? Do you agree with it now?

WORSHIP LEADERS

2

WE ARE
WORSHIPERS

Excuse me for a moment as I slip into my Captain Obvious costume for a second.

Worship leaders are worshipers.

Seems so elementary, doesn't it? And it is! It's a fundamental piece of being a Christian, and the very foundation of being a Christian leader. But I'm not so sure that we always get it.

Sure, on some level, we would all agree that we were created and redeemed to worship God. But a cursory glance at our calendars and bank accounts would show that we don't really get it. Our worship is directed elsewhere much of the time.

We are all always worshiping something or someone. We were made for it and we are exceedingly efficient at it. Our hearts are constantly on the lookout for the biggest, best, most bountiful, and most beautiful, so that we can ascribe glory to it.

It's the reason we love celebrity gossip, Instagram, and all-you-can-eat buffets. The reason we stand in line for hours to get the latest gadget. The reason Black Friday exists and the reason we spend billions each year on entertainment.

It's the reason we always have this itching feeling that the grass is greener on the other side. The reason we lust and the reason we lie. It's actually the root of all of our sins. We have a sin problem because we have a worship problem.

Romans 1:19–23 says as much.

> *For what can be known about God is plain to them, because God has shown it to them. For his invisible attributes, namely, his eternal power and divine nature, have been clearly perceived, ever since the creation of the world, in the things that have been made. So they are without excuse. For although they knew God, they did not honor him as God or give thanks to him, but they became futile in their thinking, and their foolish hearts were darkened. Claiming to be wise, they became fools, and exchanged the glory of the immortal God for images resembling mortal man and birds and animals and creeping things.*

It seems a bit silly that people would exchange God's glory to worship birds and animals and creeping things. Our worship could never be so primitive. We are far too advanced and intellectual for that.

No, nowadays we don't bow down before men or birds or cows. We just work sixty hours a week so that we can make a lot of money to buy a lot of stuff we don't need in order to impress a lot of people we don't even like that much.

We look at pornographic images and then cover them up as best as we can so that while we help ruin the broken people caught in that industry, we don't ruin our own reputations.

You know, little things like that.

Or perhaps it's not in the glaring and obvious things we can look at and quickly label as sin. We strive for comfort, power, and approval, and we find them anywhere we can, often through God's good gifts. These things aren't bad in and of themselves. God has blessed us with them for our enjoyment so that we might know His goodness and grace and then give thanks to Him. They are the shadows that point to the substance. So are family, home, and technology. We often add to that the shadows of beauty, ministry, and influence. All of these are good things, yet they can easily become functional replacements for God—the idols that drive us throughout our weeks.

Then the weekend comes and we step on the platform to lead worship at our churches and cross our fingers, hoping that the sinfulness of our secret lives will not overflow into our public ministries. What an affront to the great privilege that God has given us as leaders in His church!

Perhaps the only thing that is more outrageous than all of this is the unfathomable truth that God still delights to use us in spite of ourselves. He does this because above all things He wants to honor His Son, Jesus, who obediently came, died, and was raised to redeem us from the idols that we continually chase after.

Our secret sinfulness is in every way inexcusable. But God has excused the inexcusable in us because He put it all on the perfect Savior, Jesus, and then poured out the fullness of His wrath on Him.

This is the very definition of scandalous grace, and it is the only reason that we can repent and be free without using our freedom as an excuse to go on sinning.

Christ has appeared to crush our idols under His feet, showing Himself to be the only one worthy of worship. He has put His glory, His mercy, His compassion, and His power on display in bodily form. When we truly see who Christ is and all that He has accomplished for us, how could idols compare? How could we choose to pursue and worship those things?

We must see the contrast between our worthless idols and the infinitely worthy Savior and then take great care in choosing what or who we worship, because that is who we will become like.

Psalm 115:8 tells us that when we trust in idols, we become like the idols we trust in. I can't remember the last time I talked to someone who said, "I want to be cold and heartless. I absolutely love the idea of being powerless and idiotic." I honestly don't think I've ever met anyone who hired a life coach to help him go down that path. It is not appealing. Yet idols are heartless and powerless. And we instinctively go down this road when the good things that we ought to enjoy as gifts from God become the ultimate things that we worship as god.

I cannot fathom the inexpressible pain that countless pastors have endured as they discover their worship leaders have been engaged in long-term extramarital affairs with women in their churches. I cannot describe the grief their churches have experienced, let alone the broken homes, shattered families, and countless other victims. Add to that the way the watching world sees the church in light of situations like this, and the depth of the destructive consequences of sin grow increasingly and unavoidably obvious.

These things don't just happen overnight.

> We must see the contrast between our worthless idols and the infinitely worthy Savior.

A worship leader doesn't just wake up one day and say, "I think I'll have an affair." Over time, he makes little compromises that feed the lustful, sinful nature and begin to pile up on top of him until the convicting voice of the Holy Spirit has been completely drowned out. Tragically, that leader becomes what he never thought possible, because he worshiped comfort, approval, power, sex, and more, instead of the living God.

In contrast, 2 Corinthians 3:18 says that when we behold Jesus' glory, we are increasingly transformed into a mirror image of Him. He has freely revealed Himself to us by His Spirit so that we might worship Him, and as we worship Him we become more and more like Him. This is a great promise, but the promise is for those who behold Him. We have to think about Him. We have to spend time with Him. We have to talk with Him in prayer and hear from Him through His Word.

He is wonderful in every way and in every way wonderful to look at. Forget what your momma told you growing up. It's okay to stare. The more you stare at Him, the more you love Him; the more you worship Him, the more you become like Him.

There is a difference between a worship leader who has been intimate with Jesus in communion, meditation, and prayer all week and a worship leader who has forsaken intimacy altogether for the sake of the stimulation and pseudocommunity that social media, video games, and even porn offer.

There was a reason that the early church thrived and changed the world! Everyone recognized that the church leaders "had been with Jesus" (Acts 4:13). There is something different about people who stand often in His presence, marveling at His holiness and majesty. They walk about with the aroma of heaven on them. They have a curious confidence, a humbling humility, and a peculiar power.

That is why Jesus places such an emphasis on worshiping God in secret. It is because in the secret place, He shapes and molds us, empowers and emboldens us. When we worship Him in secret, we see things in a different light. We see ourselves, the world, and the church the way God does—the way it really is.

When we sing to God in private, there is no one there to applaud us, no one to cheer us on or tell us we are great. When we bow before God or raise our hands in private, there is no one looking on to think how humble we are, or to be impressed with how expressive we are in our praise to God. When we tear up, no one recognizes how spiritually and emotionally mature we are. There is only the perfect, holy, and wonderful God who is committed to perfecting us, and giving us more joy than we could ever comprehend, because He is making us more like the perfect, joyful Savior. And yet His presence may not be as obvious to us in private as when we are immersed in a multisensory corporate worship experience full of sound and lights and a sea of voices.

Maybe that is why our private worship seems so unfulfilling at times. Our expectations of meeting with God have become so rich and textured that the simplicity of reading God's Word for our own nourishment and edification seems insignificant. The lack of a hype-filled adrenaline rush makes the deafening silence of prayer seem mundane or boring. Maybe we forget that God is still with us in private because He is present and active in a different kind of way—not in the earthquake or the fire or the mighty rushing wind, but in the quiet whisper (see 1 Kings 19:11–13). It may not be exciting and it may not be earth shattering, so it may

> Jesus places such an emphasis on worshiping God in secret because that is where He shapes, empowers, and emboldens us.

seem backward to us that the private time is actually most significant. Yet it is absolutely indispensable.

There is something enticing, intoxicating, and even addicting about public ministry. It is very easy to be taken up with it, to be consumed by it, and to let it rule you. But public ministry won't save you. It won't transform you to be more like Christ. It won't confront you with your idols or comfort you when you fail. If you're good at it, it can lull you into a Spiritless complacency. If you're not everything people want you to be, it can crush you with condemnation.

Jesus knew that more than anyone. When everyone loved Him and crowds were constantly pressing in on Him, He intentionally and continually got away to be alone with His Father. When He was exhausted, He would pray into the darkest hours of the night or rise before the sun's first morning light. When He was facing rejection and suffering, He went to a garden or a mountain to worship God in private. He needed to be near the source of His strength and the greatest delight of His heart.

In the same way, making Jesus the greatest delight of our heart and source of our strength does not—*it cannot*—happen only when we are on stage. It is impossible to authentically "forget not . . . his benefits" (Psalms 103:2) on stage when we have failed to remind ourselves of them throughout the week. The warning of Jesus' words and the example of Jesus' life would seem to be telling us that if the only time and place we worship Jesus is on the stage, we should probably stop leading worship altogether.

The public display of worship that is not founded in and defined by the practice of regular, private worship of the risen King is hypocritical at best and demonic at worst! It screams to the world that Jesus is just the means to getting what we really want. It belittles Him of His glory, robs us of our truest joy and satisfaction, and deprives the church of the much-needed example of a leader worth emulating.

In Mark 12, the religious leaders of the day came to Jesus asking Him, "Which commandment is most important of all?"

What was His response?

"You shall love the Lord your God with all your heart and with all your soul and with all your mind and with all your strength" (Mark 12:29–30).

God's greatest desire from us is not to be the coolest musicians or the best songwriters. It's not even for us to be the best worship leaders, but rather for us to be worshipers of God. He wants the worship of Jesus' great and glorious name to be everything to us. For it to consume us, compel us, and constrain us! For our every thought and action to be taken captive by a deep, passionate, abiding affection for who God is. That in all we say and do, our lives would scream, "Not to us, O Lord, but to your name give glory!" (Ps. 115:1).

He wants the first thought of our mornings and the last thought of our evenings to be thoughts of thanksgiving and adoration for who He is and what He has done. He wants communion with us because when we commune with Him, He communicates Himself to us. He knows that He is the only great and glorious one, the only King who will not rob us and destroy us. He is the only one who does good (Romans 3:10–12), and the only one who has a good, pleasing, and acceptable will (Romans 12:1–2). He is the Father of lights in whom there is no shadow of change, and who gives every good and perfect gift (James 1:17). He

> The public display of worship that is not founded in regular private worship robs us of our truest joy and deprives the church of the example of a leader worth emulating.

is the only perfect and spotless Savior who died for His sinful, dead enemies (Ephesians 2:1–10; 1 Peter 1:18–19; Revelation 5:9–14).

We must remind ourselves of these things when we don't feel like worshiping God. We must join with David in commanding ourselves to praise the Lord, even when we don't want to. Even if it means forcing ourselves to meditate on the truth, it is the only thing that will set us free from the lie. We must turn our eyes upon Jesus and see Him for who He is—the supremely satisfying Savior—the truest, loveliest, most honorable, just, pure, commendable, and excellent One who alone is worthy of our praise (Philippians 4:8).

Make no mistake, being a worshiper will consume us. Worship demands everything from us. It changes and transforms us. As we worship, we cease to be who we were before. The old person continues to gradually pass away each day, and the new continues to come in greater measure.

This will happen no matter what we are worshiping. If we worship money, we will become greedy misers. If we worship fame, we will become arrogant narcissists. If we worship comfort, approval, or power, we will become like the thing we worship—and it will destroy us! The undue worship of those lesser things will feed the sinful man and eventually lead to death in our lives.

But Jesus promises that when we worship Him above all things, we will have abundant life and that He will produce in us the fruit of love, joy, peace, patience, kindness, goodness, faithfulness, gentleness, and self-control. He promises that when we worship the Way, the Truth, and the Life, in the end we will not be lost, cheated, or

> We must turn our eyes upon Jesus and see Him for who He is—the truest, loveliest, most honorable, just, pure, commendable, and excellent One.

destroyed. When we come to Him weary and burdened, He will give us rest. He promises to dine with us and give us a share in the victory He won on our behalf over those lesser things that we might be tempted to worship and the death that they bring!

When we look at worship in this way, the only obvious choice is that we would be worshipers of Jesus. And we should never be ashamed to forsake all other things in order to go for the obvious choice. We may need to remind ourselves from time to time that it's obvious for a reason, but we will never regret refusing to worship anything other than Jesus in order to worship Him alone.

QUESTIONS FOR LEADERS

1. What steps do you take to nourish a healthy private life of worship?

2. What are the hindrances to you spending time with Jesus in private worship daily? What will you do about this?

3. Have you ever sung to God in private, where "there is no one ... to applaud [you], no one to cheer [you] on or tell [you you] are great"? If you have, how did you feel? If you have not, why not?

4. When we don't feel like worshiping God, we should remind ourselves of His many noble qualities, says the author, including His goodness, His unchanging nature (or *immutability*), His truthfulness, His love, His justice, His purity, and His excellence. Which of these do you most appreciate in your Father? Spend time meditating on that quality and thank Him for it.

WORSHIP LEADERS

WE ARE
REDEEMED & ADOPTED

Some years ago, I was beyond frustrated serving in a church where I felt I was running on a hamster wheel. Week after week I would "lead worship," but it never seemed to elicit the response I hoped for. The people stood bored, uninspired, and generally apathetic, keeping their hands in pockets and their arms folded. I was rarely thanked or encouraged, and it seemed I was wasting my time.

At the same time, I would frequently travel to lead worship for conferences and concerts where my band would be paid well, fed well, put up in nice hotels, and constantly thanked and praised for our great work. When we led worship, people raised their hands and voices and sang loudly. Afterward, we would sign autographs, sell CDs and

T-shirts, and take pictures with our "biggest fans." I wanted more.

So I began to push. And push some more. I booked up my schedule to the brim and worked incessantly to force open as many doors as possible for me to make a name for myself. It became an obsession and, consequently, a huge point of tension in my marriage.

My wife and I argued all the time.

Of course, I knew just enough Bible to be dangerous, so when she lovingly came to me to tell me that it seemed like I was getting off track, I would get frustrated and annoyed, insist she was wrong, and then invent some hyperspiritual sounding excuse explaining how all of my motivations were actually for the glory of God. I had deceived my own heart and foolishly thought I was deceiving her.

Finally, one day, in the middle of an argument over the whole thing, I shouted to Amanda, "All I'm ever going to be is a local church worship leader!" As I heard the words leave my mouth, I felt God's heart break. In the depths of my soul, I could feel the Holy Spirit begin His work of conviction in me. He brought Ephesians 5:26–27 to mind to remind me that the church is the bride for whom Christ gave Himself up, rather than a stepping-stone for my own fame and glory. John 10 reminded me that the church are His sheep, and they need a shepherd not a rock star.

I was undone.

And then, because of His kindness, God used the wrecking ball of Psalm 46:10 to tear down the walls of strife I was experiencing from working toward the exaltation of the wrong name. "Be still and know that I am God. *I* will be exalted among the nations" (italics added). Finally Ephesians 1:5–8 comforted me as an adopted son of God, who was purchased by the blood of Christ and blessed beyond comprehension.

Until that moment, I hadn't realized that I had been searching for worth in things that could not give it, for satisfaction in broken wells. I was subconsciously using people to find validation, trying to create a better identity than the one I had been given in Christ. When people didn't cooperate with my plans, I got frustrated with them, rather than humbly serving them as their pastor.

We all have those moments when we struggle to get past our own selfish, fleshly impulses of wanting to be great. We may never want to admit it, but if we took some time to stop and pray and ask God to show us, we'd see it's there.

Even the disciples had this issue. In Luke 9:46–48, we find them bickering with one another about who is greatest.

> An argument arose among them as to which of them was
> the greatest. But Jesus, knowing the reasoning of their
> hearts, took a child and put him by his side and said to
> them, "Whoever receives this child in my name receives
> me, and whoever receives me receives him who sent me.
> For he who is least among you all is the one who is great."

I find it intriguing that Jesus, the God who created them, and the very definition of true greatness, was there in His disciples' midst. He stood there listening to them argue about which one of them was greater. And yet because He knew His disciples' natural inclinations and reasoning, He was very patient with them as He told them how to truly be great.

He didn't say, "If a door isn't opening, try a little harder. If that doesn't work, kick it down." He said to serve people. To be last. But they just didn't get it.

Like the disciples, we have a fundamentally flawed understanding of greatness that says our worth and significance is found in what we do and how well we do it. So we jockey for position and obsess over trying to make ourselves worthy, when Jesus alone can do that for us.

It's like we're a bunch of Uncle Rico's running around!

In the movie *Napoleon Dynamite*, Uncle Rico is a middle-aged man who has been paralyzed from doing anything significant with his life because he has become obsessed with the constant inner nagging that if he just had another shot, he could have made state in high school football.

If the team had been state champions, he would have made something of himself … but instead he lives in a van and mooches off of people while selling Tupperware, breast enhancement drugs, and any get-rich-quick scheme he can get his hands on.

He put his identity and worth in something that seems outrageous to the average person, but because things didn't go his way, he ceased to believe he could make a significant contribution to the world. He became what most would call a "loser." If you saw the movie, you would probably agree.

While it's easy to point out Uncle Rico's fatal flaw, it may not be quite as obvious that we are all prone to doing this kind of thing. God has given each of us unique talents and ambitions and personalities, and because we are fallen human beings, we all tend to gravitate toward finding our worth in these things instead of in who we are in Christ.

We use our newly formed, self-appointed identities to cover our brokenness and faults, and to recommend ourselves to each other and to God.

But it is never enough. There will always be someone else who is more talented and successful. So we play the comparison game and covet other people's talents and success, because if we could just be like that, we could check off the list at the end of the day and call it a job well done. We would be complete. We could be happy.

Very few are content to be faithful with

> We play the comparison game and covet other people's talents and success, because if we could just be like that, we think we would be complete.

what God has given them. They drive and drive and push and push to prove themselves and create their own identity in the image of whoever they think is occupying the place they should be standing.

Allow me to put an end to this game: God does not have one ounce of concern to make you like that person you keep comparing yourself to. He doesn't want to form you into their image. He wants to form you into the image of His Son, who loved you and gave Himself up for you!

That's right: He wants to form you into the image of pure holiness, satisfaction, joy, peace, and love.

When Jesus, the humble servant of all, said that if we would be the greatest, we must be the least, He was saying, "This kind of counter-cultural, counterintuitive living takes a humility that can only come from one place."

To put yourself last and be a servant of all people is the kind of lifestyle that can spring forth only from an internalized realization and practical application of your standing before God. It means that you know that no matter how hard you try, no identity that you can create is better than the one that God has given you in Christ.

We will never be more noticed, loved, cherished, accepted, validated, encouraged, and satisfied than we are in Christ. We will never have a greater identity than the one He has purchased for us on the cross. We are created in the image of God, bought with His blood, and redeemed for His glory. Greater still, He adopted us into His family and gave us an eternal inheritance, a new family, and the Holy Spirit to dwell in us!

Let that sink in for a moment. Do you have any idea what a huge privilege it is to be adopted into the family of God?

> No identity that you can create is better than the one that God has given you in Christ.

In his book *Knowing God*, J. I. Packer says of our adoption in Christ:

> *Adoption is the highest privilege that the gospel offers: higher even than justification. . . . That justification—by which we mean God's forgiveness of the past together with His acceptance for the future—is the primary and fundamental blessing of the gospel is not in question. Justification is the primary blessing, because it meets our primary spiritual need. We all stand by nature under God's judgment; His law condemns us; guilt gnaws at us, making us restless, miserable, and in our lucid moments afraid; we have no peace in ourselves, because we have not peace with our Maker. So we need the forgiveness of our sins, and assurance of a restored relationship with God, more than we need anything else in the world; and this the gospel offers us before it offers us anything else. . . . And as justification is the primary blessing, so it is the fundamental blessing, in the sense that everything else in our salvation assumes it, and rests on it—adoption included.*

> *But this is not to say that justification is the highest blessing of the gospel. Adoption is higher, because of the richer relationship with God that it involves. . . . Justification is a forensic idea, conceived in terms of law, and viewing God as judge. . . . Adoption is a family idea, conceived in terms of love, and viewing God as father. In adoption, God takes us into His family and fellowship, and establishes us as His children and heirs. Closeness, affection and generosity are at the heart of the relationship. To be right with God*

*the judge is a great thing, but to be loved and cared for
by God the father is a greater.*[1]

On July 7, 2011, my wife and I brought home our two adopted sons from Ethiopia. The excruciatingly drawn-out eighteen months leading up to that moment was filled with a seemingly impossible amount of fund-raising, waiting, mountains of paperwork, background checks, waiting, education, waiting, and trying to stay calm as we explained to people who just couldn't understand why we were adopting when we already had two biological children.

Plus, did I mention all the waiting?

Finally, the time came for us to fly to Ethiopia. So we left our two girls with their grandma and went to the homeland of our soon-to-be sons. As we sat in the courtroom in Ethiopia, the judge asked us a few short questions.

"Will you love these boys the way you love your biological children?"

"Yes."

"Will you give these boys the same inheritance you will give your biological children?"

"Yes."

"You realize this is completely irreversible? Nothing you can do and nothing they can do can make them no longer your sons . . . ?"

"Yes."

"Then, Mr. and Mrs. Miller, they are yours."

They escorted us out and gave us our sons' new, official birth certificates. We were their parents. They were our sons. My name was their new name. It was legally irreversible.

As soon as our boys were in their new home, in their own beds, with their new family and their new names, we could barely remember how hard it had been. They were ours. We were theirs.

Previously they didn't have the love of a family, but now they did. They didn't choose us; we chose them. They didn't earn their way into our family and they could do nothing to earn their way out. There is no way they could make me stop loving them, fighting for them, or providing for them. I love them both the same way I love my daughters, and the four children all have the same benefits. There is absolutely nothing they can do to change that.

I don't know that I will ever fully understand my adoption in Christ this side of eternity, and yet I don't think that anything has shown me what an indescribable privilege it is more than adopting our two boys. It is incredible to me how much it has changed my outlook on being a worship leader.

We were dead in our sins. We were slaves. We were orphans. *But God*— the perfect, sovereign, holy Creator God over all the universe—"being rich in mercy, because of the great love with which he loved us . . . made us alive together with Christ" (Ephesians 2:4–5). He chose us. He forgave us. He redeemed us from our sins and sinfulness. He made us just as if we had never sinned. But He didn't stop there.

He took us in His arms and adopted us and decided to love us the same way He loves Jesus. He gave us the same inheritance He gives Jesus. He gave us a new eternal home where we will live with Him forever and enjoy who He is. Now He calls us His sons and daughters and we call Him Father.

So God has given us a new name. He also has given us a new family—the church.

We didn't earn any of this. We had earned death. We had earned hell. But He did all of this because He wanted to. Because He loves us. All this is not based upon our performance, but based on His own.

> God chose us.
> He forgave us.
> He redeemed us
> from our sins
> and sinfulness.
> But He didn't
> stop there.
> He took us in
> His arms and
> adopted us.

WE ARE REDEEMED & ADOPTED

As I look at my adoption in Christ, I see with a greater clarity that no amount of being the perfect worship leader secured this standing for me. No measure of being a good vocalist or songwriter caused Him to choose me and love me.

How freeing it is to know that God's redemptive, adopting love is not contingent upon us but upon Himself. Though we often want to act like orphans who don't have a loving Father to provide what's best for us, this could not be further from the truth. Though we are fickle and wobbly in our love for Him, He is steadfast and unwavering in His love for us because we are hidden in Christ and accepted by God! We are complete in Him.

Many of us serve sacrificially, week after week, and have never been noticed or applauded. We are not successful by the world's standards. We seek acceptance from the people we lead and serve, but instead find grumbling and complaining about what people didn't like rather than the affirmation our souls so eagerly desire. This is not to say the grumbling and complaining or lack of encouragement is okay.

This is to say that we are okay without commendation. For we are commended by God.

So we don't need to have people raise their hands and sing loud in corporate worship. We don't need to have them come to us later to say how great worship was. We don't need to grow our platform, have a well-read blog, go on tour, lead worship at the biggest conferences, or have the top-selling Christian album on iTunes.

We have God Himself, in the person of Jesus, by whom we are redeemed and adopted. And that is more than enough.

QUESTIONS FOR LEADERS

1. In what ways are you attempting to create an identity for yourself?

2. What about yourself do you think is most important? What do you lead with when you introduce yourself? What do you want everyone to know about you?

3. As believers, you and I are commended by, loved by, and adopted by God. Can you think of anything you have done or any logical reason why God would do this?

4. How does the fact God has adopted you impact the way you view God and yourself?

WORSHIP LEADERS

4

PASTORS & DEACONS

At some point in the early 2000s, the modern worship movement really took off. I'm not exactly sure when or how it happened, but we have come a long way from having just a few choices when it comes to how we worship. The Christian music industry is now largely driven by the writing and production of corporate worship music.

For a while the popular Christian music trend was the compilation disc, which featured the most popular Christian artists of the day performing the most popular corporate worship songs of the day. Those CDs had paid advertising slots on late-night Christian television, were released in a series of volumes, and had some pretty hilarious names, like "The Greatest Worship Hits 17," "Worship Songs 28," and "The Most

Incredible Worship Songs, Volume 84." The TV programs promoted them with lines like, "These are seriously the most incredible worship songs ever—seriously!"

Perhaps I'm exaggerating a bit. I don't think any of them actually got to an 84th volume. Maybe a 52nd, but 80 would have been overdoing things. Nonetheless, the trend revolutionized the way people thought about Christian music. In some ways, this helped to expand the glory of God in the minds of believers all over the world, yet we also simplified the worship of God to what could be bought and sold in the market and forced performing artists to become worship leaders if they wanted to keep selling albums.

But the Bible never says that being able to sing and play an instrument qualifies someone to lead His church. In fact, the reputation that is most frequently associated with artists and musicians these days is opposite to the qualifications of a leader as outlined in the New Testament.

Ephesians 4:11–12 outlines what leadership of his church looks like: "And he gave the apostles, the prophets, the evangelists, the shepherds and teachers, to equip the saints for the work of ministry, for building up the body of Christ."

Apostle. Prophet. Evangelist. Shepherd. Teacher. These are the roles of leadership within the New Testament church. Significantly, worship leader is not listed. Neither is musician or singer. Yet the majority of corporate worship services are prominently led by musicians. This is a ton of influence over the church for a position that is not even listed in the Ephesians 4:11 leadership grid. There must be more to this role than simply playing songs with excellence.

While there has been some disagreement among theologians through the history of the church as to whether this list is exhaustive, it is safe to assume that the worship leader falls into one of the aforementioned leadership categories. While it is possible that the worship leader could fit into any of them to some degree, it is most common in the context of the local church that the worship leader would act as a type of pastor/teacher.

When a worship leader leads the church in corporate worship through singing, he or she is taking on the role of Christ's undershepherd, helping to create an atmosphere and environment where people can meet with God and find spiritual refreshing and nourishment.

By deciding which songs the local church sings, a worship leader is exercising his pastoral responsibility. He must discern the doctrines he is teaching to whomever he is leading and shepherd them into a greater understanding of gospel truth.

Every time he calls his people to worship and leads them in praise, thanksgiving, and adoration of God's glory and holiness; every time he guides them in confession of their sins, assures them of their unshakeable salvation because of Christ's death on the cross and His resurrection; every time he exhorts them in light of those things to commit themselves to live on mission for God's fame in the world, he is building the gospel into them. Using psalms, hymns, and spiritual songs, the worship leader is giving them the spiritual food that they desperately need.

This is not to say that the worship leader is acting autonomously. He is leading in concert with the pastors/elders of the church, submitting to the lead elder or senior pastor. Therefore, while in a teaching role, he may not necessarily be serving in the office of pastor/elder.

There is another office found in Scripture that is not listed in the Ephesians 4:11 leadership grid, perhaps because it is not a governing role but rather a serving one. It is the role of deacon.

The word *deacon* comes from the Greek word *diakonos*, which simply means one who serves. In Acts 6, we see that the first deacons in the church were appointed because a need arose regarding provision for widows who were being overlooked. The apostles knew that all throughout the Scriptures true religion had been defined by God as looking after widows and orphans in their distress, and that justice was a worship issue. Yet they didn't feel they should get distracted from their primary pastoral responsibilities of preaching God's Word and prayer, so they appointed godly men of character and integrity who could attend to the specific needs of the church.

Moving forward from that point, we find that throughout the New Testament and church history, men and women have served as deacons in order to care for the people, needs, and ministries within the church. The needs of congregations have changed with time, culture, and circumstances, and so the service of the deacons has been very fluid to be able to change with those needs.

The New Testament authors give us specific instructions for singing within the context of an orderly corporate worship gathering (1 Corinthians 14:13–40, Ephesians 5:19, Colossians 3:16). In order to maintain the orderliness of the gathering and to guard the integrity of the content from the heresies of the day, a pastor/elder would have been in charge of either leading this gathering or appointing, leading, and overseeing a deacon as he performed this duty to meet this spiritual need of the church.

But not just anyone could be a pastor or deacon. The apostles didn't just grab anyone who was a good public speaker and immediately appoint him to preach, or anyone who was good with money and immediately appoint him or her to take care of collecting the offerings. In the same way, they would have never just pulled in a guy who could sing pretty well and immediately given him the responsibility of leading the singing within the church without any theological discipleship or lifestyle requirements. They gave specific guidelines of what kind of people could be pastors and who could be deacons.

We see these guidelines in 1 Timothy 3:1–13, the qualifications for elders and deacons:

The saying is trustworthy: If anyone aspires to the office of overseer, he desires a noble task. Therefore an overseer must be above reproach, the husband of one wife, sober-minded, self-controlled, respectable, hospitable, able to teach, not a drunkard, not violent but gentle, not quarrelsome, not a lover of money. He must manage his own household well, with all dignity keeping his children submissive, for if someone does not know how to manage his own household, how will he care for God's church? He must not be a recent convert, or he may become puffed up with conceit and fall into the condemnation of the devil. Moreover, he must be well thought of by outsiders, so that he may not fall into disgrace, into a snare of the devil.

Deacons likewise must be dignified, not double-tongued, not addicted to much wine, not greedy for dishonest gain. They must hold the mystery of the faith with a clear conscience. And let them also be tested first; then let them serve as deacons if they prove themselves blameless. Their wives likewise must be dignified, not slanderers, but sober-minded, faithful in all things. Let deacons each be the husband of one wife, managing their children and their own households well. For those who serve well as deacons gain a good standing for themselves and also great confidence in the faith that is in Christ Jesus.

Then again in Titus 1:5–9, we see further instructions for choosing pastors.

> Appoint elders in every town as I directed you—if anyone is
> above reproach, the husband of one wife, and his children
> are believers and not open to the charge of debauchery or
> insubordination. For an overseer, as God's steward, must
> be above reproach. He must not be arrogant or quick-
> tempered or a drunkard or violent or greedy for gain, but
> hospitable, a lover of good, self-controlled, upright, holy,
> and disciplined. He must hold firm to the trustworthy word
> as taught, so that he may be able to give instruction in
> sound doctrine and also to rebuke those who contradict it.

J. Oswald Sanders, in his book *Spiritual Leadership*, breaks down these qualifications into six key categories.[1]

→ *Social qualifications.* Above reproach, with a good reputation among unbelievers. Dignified. Displays a holy and joyful life. Respected by others.

→ *Moral qualifications.* Not arrogant. Not greedy or a lover of money. Not in ministry for dishonest gain. Above reproach. Not a slanderer or liar. Faithful to his spouse. Temperate (having self-control).

→ *Mental qualifications.* Able to teach sound doctrine and rebuke false teachers. Hold the mystery of the faith (have a good grasp of the gospel). A well-ordered mind, which results in a well-ordered life.

→ *Disposition (personality) qualifications.* Genial, considerate, and gentle. Self-controlled and disciplined. Given to hospitality. Not quick-tempered, violent, or quarrelsome. Not a drunk.

→ *Domestic qualifications.* Husband of one wife (not a ladies' man or flirtatious). Able to manage his family well. Has spiritual aspiration as he leads his spouse and family.

→ *Maturity.* Not a new convert. Able to teach. Tested—has had opportunities to serve in less prominent tasks that have developed both natural and spiritual gifts. Faithful. Sober-minded. Holy. Upright.

The qualifications of elder and deacon are practically identical, with the exception of being able to teach (required of elders only). Yet even there, a deacon must have a comprehensive understanding of life and a lifestyle that reflects the mystery of the gospel. Notice it doesn't say a deacon cannot teach. He is just not required to.

The bar has been set high for the qualifications of leaders within God's church who represent Him in their teaching, service, and lifestyles worthy of imitation. Those who aspire to lead and teach must measure up and know that they will be judged more strictly as those who are accountable to keep watch over God's church (James 3:1; Hebrews 13:17).

A worship leader is not just a singer or musician or artist. He is not a marketing guru or someone who knows what music people like. He is a pastor or deacon; a servant, a steward, and watchman over God's church. He is a teacher of doctrine, accountable to God for his teaching and his life. He must hold this in tension, being neither puffed up by his position or thinking of his role as less important than it is. It is an immense privilege and responsibility to lead God's church, and there are many who are

> A worship leader is not just a singer or musician or artist. He is a pastor or deacon, and watchman over God's church. He is a teacher of doctrine.

leading who do not meet these qualifications. Yet as Paul encourages, "If anyone aspires to the office of overseer, he desires a noble task."

To lead worship is a noble aspiration, worth wholeheartedly pursuing. But we must pursue it on God's terms. We must first become people of godly character and integrity who love Jesus and His church more than our own glory, fame, and prestige. We must be more concerned with people knowing Christ than knowing us, and more in love with His name than with our own. If that were the pastoral heart, motivation, and expectation behind every worship leader's efforts, then I imagine the worship of Jesus Christ would be a lot more than the best ten songs out there done and redone by every famous artist. It would be a movement that would change the world.

QUESTIONS FOR LEADERS

1. "A worship leader is not just a singer or musician or artist. He is a pastor or deacon, and watchman over God's church. He is a teacher of doctrine." Do you agree with these statements that as a worship leader you have a pastoral or diaconal role, and that you are to guard the purity of the church and teach doctrine as opportunities arise? Why or why not?

2. Do you meet the qualifications of a pastor or deacon found in Scripture? If not, what will you do about it?

3. What ways are you intentionally shepherding and pastoring people in your worship leading?

4. Based on the final paragraph of this chapter, which of these areas do you need to work on to be a more effective worship leader? (You may choose more than one area.) Then in private prayer or with a group, pray that God through His Spirit would help you to grow and mature in this area(s).

   ☐ Become a person of godly character.

   ☐ Become a person of integrity.

   ☐ Learn to love Jesus and His church more than my own glory.

   ☐ Help people to know Christ better.

WORSHIP LEADERS

5.

WE ARE
THEOLOGIANS

No matter your age, you should recall the melody to this classic children's song: A B C D E F G . . . H I J K L M N O P . . . You're singing along, aren't you? Sing with me—Q R S . . . T U V . . . W X . . . Y and Z.

You remember the song, right? The catchiness of its melody was responsible for fusing into your brain some of the most foundational facts you have ever learned. And not just the facts themselves, but the memories and very experience of learning them.

I still remember learning my ABCs in preschool. I remember the brand-new, multicolored mats we sat on as the teacher introduced us to the large, plush-doll cartoon characters that were shaped as each letter. Each one had his own theme song that he sang on tape. As I recall, *F* was tall and lanky and sported a set of size 23 early '80s Chuck Taylors as he sang his theme song, "Feet, Happy Feet." *T* was short and stocky and his teeth spanned the breadth of his entire body as he sang his theme song, "Teeth, Tall Teeth." It stuck with me. I can still sing those songs today.

I remember going to church as a child and learning to sing, "Jesus loves me, this I know" and "Jesus loves the little children of the world" and actually believing the truth as I sang it for all to hear. I learned that God had a plan to show His love to the world through me as I sang, "This little light of mine, I'm gonna let it shine."

Those simple songs were the bedrock for my childlike faith. If no one else loved me, I knew Jesus did.

Even as a child, songs were constantly shaping my theology. They were shaping my love for Jesus, teaching me who He is and what He has done. They made me a worshiper.

As an adult, it is no different. I can look at some of the other songs I learned growing up and see how they have formed me as a Christian. I remember how some of the broken theology in them unintentionally gave me permission to become a selfish, human-centered Christian because they made Jesus look like a weak God whose universe centered around me. Sigh. Even then, poor theology had me grasping at half-truths and no truths at all. Today correct theology remains the power of the music we choose to lead or even write. As a child, those lyrics would shape the way I viewed Jesus for years to come.

Other songs I would sing boasted of the glory and holiness of God in a way that I could not ignore or deny. The truth in those songs would eventually win out and demolish all the lies I had believed about God before. Those songs were foundational and I still sing them to this day.

God gave us the gift of music. He created it with unique properties for our enjoyment, expression, edification, and education.

This is not to downplay the formative importance of preaching in the church, but honestly I could not tell you the take-home point of two sermons I heard growing up, no matter how clever the preacher's alliteration was. But I can still sing "Holy, Holy, Holy" word for word. I know "Great Is Thy Faithfulness" by heart. "The Solid Rock" is an ever-present companion for me in difficult times. Those songs have taught me a vocabulary to express myself when I come before God, and in that expression to learn the truth of God in a way that will stay with me for a lifetime.

We don't need to perform scientific studies to see that music and melody fuse truth into our memories and intellects in a unique way. We can all observe how melody attaches meaning, emotions, affections, and experiences to words like nothing else can. How it takes phrases and sentences to new heights and depths that they couldn't go on their own. We tend to remember the seasons of our lives by the soundtrack of that season, partly because the soundtrack actually shapes the seasons of our lives. The thoughts we dwell on, the truths we listen to—all of these shape our worldview and make us who we are.

This is true spiritually. The songs we sing teach us theology. For better or worse, as worship leaders, the songs we

> Melody attaches meaning, emotions, affections, and experiences to words like nothing else can. It takes phrases to heights that they couldn't go on their own.

choose to sing with our churches will inevitably shape the way they view God and interact with Him. Songs that are rich with gospel truth and weighty in God-centered, Christ-honoring content will shape worshipers who understand and adore God, while deficient, flimsy, man-centered songs will produce a lack of understanding of who God actually is, which leads to deficient, flimsy, man-centered worship. If we are to worship God, we must know who He really is.

My wife is a petite, green-eyed, blonde-haired, gorgeous woman. She is kind and compassionate, loves our children, and is an incredible mother and wife. I could go on and on about all of the things that I love about her.

But what if I were to come to her and say, "I wrote this song for you to tell you how much I love you"—and then went on to sing about how much I love her brunette hair and brown eyes and how I can't wait to marry her and have kids someday? She would be confused and would maybe wonder if I wrote the song about another woman.

Or what if that song was actually all about me? A tribute to myself, how she makes me feel, and how I must be so great that she would love me? I praise her for being smart enough to choose to spend the rest of her life with me, because I'm the center of the universe and she is lucky to have me.

I'll tell you what she'd do. She would be offended and might make me go to counseling to get a better handle on reality. And she would be right! I would have to be a lunatic to do something like that.

We do this very thing to God when we blatantly or unintentionally disregard the prominent presence of God's Word in the songs we sing and are flippant about the words that we sing to Him and about Him. When we ascribe to Him attributes and motives that are not true to who He is, or sing "to Him" songs that only exalt ourselves, we aren't in touch with reality anymore, regardless of how good our intentions might be.

I often wonder if sometimes, when we are singing to God in corporate worship, He is listening and thinking, "Who do they think they are singing about? Because it's certainly not Me!"

Worship leaders have the responsibility to make sure this doesn't happen. As I said in the last chapter, we have a unique teaching role within the church. We are telling people who God is and how He has acted through the songs that we sing. That means that we have to actually know Him. We have to be students of the Scriptures and diligently pursue relationship with Him and a knowledge of Him.

We must be theologians.

A theologian is someone who makes it his life's mission to know God's nature, character, will, and ways with the highest level of expertise possible. A theologian is a warrior shepherd who knows God's truth, instructs in God's truth, and fights for God's truth in the church. Who holds "firm to the trustworthy word as taught, so that he may be able to give instruction in sound doctrine and also to rebuke those who contradict it" (Titus 1:9).

When we are leading our people in worship through singing, we are actually putting words into their mouths to sing to God. Therefore, it is imperative that we guard with all diligence the songs that we choose for our people to sing and be careful to maintain the doctrinal integrity of the content we are teaching. It must be truth in song every time. No exceptions.

As a student of the God who has revealed Himself in the Bible, a worship leader must prayerfully examine what each song is teaching and ask the question, "Is this true according to what God has revealed about Himself in Scripture?" This doesn't necessarily mean that it has to be word for word from the Bible, but it should conform to what we find there. We simply can't improve on what God has to say about God. He is the ultimate authority on Himself. There are many songs out there, both old and new, that are absolute nonsense when it comes to speaking about God rightly and coherently, and we must humbly, prayerfully, and intentionally weed these out.

Additionally, we must ask, "Is this song making much of me or of God?" God is very passionate about His glory. He will not give it to another (Isaiah 48:11). Yet we are prone to mistaking sentimental or emotional experiences with the type of worship that God desires from us; namely, worship that is in spirit and truth.

The world is constantly spewing lies to us.

"You deserve it."

"You earned it."

"You have to look out for Number One."

"You have to love YOURSELF first."

"You have to do whatever makes YOU happy."

In all of these subtle ways the world tells us that it's all about us. Those lies start to creep into our personal lives and we begin to compromise the truth. We exchange the glory of the Creator for the created and eventually replace God with ourselves. And as we become the object of our own worship, these subtleties start to creep into our worship services. They creep into our songs and the way we interpret and preach Scripture. They creep in as a consumer mentality that says we must bend over backwards to please the consumer Christians who are attending.

As theologians, we must be able to lead away from the cultural norms and engage the emotions and affections of people with the truth that God alone is worthy of our worship. We must make sure that the songs we sing with our church focus on the attributes, character, and actions of God—His power, majesty, glory, justice, mercy, compassion, and greatness. There will never be a shortage of things to focus on here.

The best news in the world is that God wants us to know Him! He is a loving Father who wants what is best for us, and in His grace, patience, and compassion, He has chosen to reveal His will and His ways to us through His Word. If we would know God and teach His ways in our songs, we must love His Word. We must read it, study it, memorize it, meditate on it, and live it.

But this will not come with a light cursory skimming of the Scriptures whenever we feel like it. It will not come by washing over the parts of the Bible that we don't like or understand. Neither will it come by attempting to candy-coat the hard truths in order to make them more palatable, nor by twisting its words to make it mean what we want it to. We cannot neglect to read God's Word because we are too busy, don't understand it, or don't enjoy it. If we are to know God, if we are to delight in Him and lead people in that delight, we must know Scripture.

Jonathan Edwards says of God's Word, "This is the fountain from which all knowledge in Divinity must be derived. Therefore, let not this treasure lie by you neglected."[1]

God's Word is our treasure. It is paramount and is to take prominence in our studying. At the same time, we must not be arrogant in thinking that we have it down, or that every idea we think about God must be original. We have the benefit of living in a time where information and education is more accessible than ever.

> The songs we sing with our church must focus on the attributes, character, and actions of God— His power, majesty, glory, justice, mercy, compassion, and greatness.

At the click of a computer mouse button (or smart phone, PC tablet, or e-reader download for that matter), we can read the greatest works by theologians and historians of the last two thousand years.

Jonathan Edwards himself was a theologian who often spent fourteen hours per day studying the Scriptures. Today we can glean much from his studies, as well as from those of many other spiritual fathers who have gone before us. To say the least, the words and works of Athanasius, Augustine, Martin Luther, John Calvin, Charles Spurgeon, A. W. Tozer, and C. S. Lewis ought to occupy a large chunk of our studies of the living God, as well as reading from such contemporary Christian thinkers and theologians as John Piper, Timothy Keller, Wayne Grudem, J. I. Packer, and R. C. Sproul.

Fiction is good. Leadership books are fine. Self-help or how-to readings—sure. But learning from these spiritual giants who have gone before us should occupy the worship leader's reading more than anything but the Bible itself. We must dare to think their thoughts, test their works, and apply their writings where appropriate. We must work to let the deep truths of their labor in theology shape the way we relate to God as well as the way we relate to the church in the songs we sing and the way we sing them.

We must drench our worship in doctrine and saturate our services and songs in Scripture. In doing so, we will lay a strong theological foundation on which the Lord will build His kingdom. He will be lifted up and draw men to Himself. After all, to borrow a phrase from the song that taught you your left from your right, "that's what it's all about."

QUESTIONS FOR LEADERS

1. What great Christian hymns and/or worship songs help you to personally know God and His Son better? What do you really like about these hymns or songs? Sing one of these songs to God the Father or Son today and a second one later in the week as part of your quiet time with God.

2. Based on the truth of their content, are there any songs in your corporate worship repertoire that you need to drop? Any that you need to add?

3. What attributes of God do you appreciate the most? What songs, choruses, and hymns do you and your worship team use that spotlight those truths about God?

4. How frequently do you read the Bible, study it, memorize it, and meditate on it? If it not regularly, what keeps you from having a consist time in the reading and study of God's Word?

WORSHIP LEADERS

WE ARE
STORYTELLERS
(LITURGISTS)

One of my favorite movies of all time is the holiday masterpiece *Elf*. It's hilarious and heartwarming, and I think I could watch it year-round based on those two factors alone.

In the movie, Walter Hobbs is a cynical, heartless New York City publishing executive who discovers that a particular children's book his company has printed is missing a page that contains some significant plot details. His response is to ignore the problem and ship the book anyway, as to avoid "taking a $30,000 bath so some kid can understand what happened to a puppy and a frigging pigeon."

Later on in the movie, we see the fallout of this terrible decision when Walter's boss comes to visit him, fuming! His niece wants to know "how a certain puppy and a certain pigeon escape the clutches of a certain evil witch," but the book is missing these important details.

Great stories are meant to be told! And told in the fullness of their key plotlines and dialogue. We can never fully appreciate the story when we miss out on those key elements. There are even phone apps now to help you not miss major points of a movie in the case of a restroom emergency. The integrity of the story is at stake if you miss them!

Worship leaders are storytellers. Every song we sing tells a story. But even beyond that, the order of the songs, the way those songs are sung, and the other elements of the corporate worship service are telling the story! This storytelling is called the liturgy.

Some people get scared away by the word *liturgy*. I confess I was once one of these people. When I heard the word *liturgy*, I thought of a group of people lifelessly standing in a room robotically reciting meaningless words in a sort of "Pledge of Allegiance" type way. While there are certainly forms of lifeless, robotic liturgies out there, liturgy itself is not inherently passionless or boring. It is a storytelling tool—a framework.

In fact, the word *liturgy* simply means the ordering of worship. It is the systematic, thoughtful programming of telling the gospel story in and through the songs and other elements of a worship service. Every church has a liturgy. Every time a person worships at a church, he is worshiping within some liturgical context, some ordering of thoughts. It's simply a matter of which one.

For the first many years of my life as a worship leader, I simply wrote out a "set list" of doctrinally rich songs that helped to strengthen the message of the teaching pastor, preferably in like keys so that I could have good, smooth transitions. Yet there was a whole other dimension of storytelling that I was missing out on.

I was neglecting the glaring opportunity to retell the gospel not only with each individual song, but with the order in which I did those songs. As a result, I would unintentionally leave entire portions of the gospel story untold each week.

Without the framework of a liturgy, it is easy to naturally gravitate toward what we are good at. Some worship leaders are great at praise and adoration, but fail to ever call their people to repent or to be on mission. And some are so mission-focused that they leave Christ and His work out of the service altogether! Others are naturally confessional, and a service becomes depressingly me-centered, focusing completely on sin and suffering, while forgetting to joyfully express praise and adoration to our holy God for His grace and mercy.

A well thought-out liturgy forces us as worship leaders to face our weaknesses and grow in the gospel, while enabling us to form our people in the whole truth of the Scriptures. But where do we find a liturgy like that? One might start with the Bible itself!

God's Word is full of examples where people encounter God in worship. Revelation is bursting with adoration of the King. The Psalms give us a great framework as well. In fact, the entire Bible could be viewed as one big liturgy of the creation, fall, redemption, and restoration of mankind and how God has and is graciously and intentionally interacting with us at every point.

Thousands of historic and biblical liturgies are out there for different seasons and situations, and plenty of great resources exist to help you find them, yet the primary liturgy that I have chosen to employ on a weekly basis is an incredibly helpful one that pastors have been using since the earliest days of the church. It comes from Isaiah 6:1–8.

> *In the year that King Uzziah died I saw the Lord sitting*
> *upon a throne, high and lifted up; and the train of his*
> *robe filled the temple. Above him stood the seraphim.*

Each had six wings: with two he covered his face, and with two he covered his feet, and with two he flew. And one called to another and said: "Holy, holy, holy is the Lord of hosts; the whole earth is full of his glory!"

And the foundations of the thresholds shook at the voice of him who called, and the house was filled with smoke. And I said: "Woe is me! For I am lost; for I am a man of unclean lips, and I dwell in the midst of a people of unclean lips; for my eyes have seen the King, the Lord of hosts!"

Then one of the seraphim flew to me, having in his hand a burning coal that he had taken with tongs from the altar. And he touched my mouth and said: "Behold, this has touched your lips; your guilt is taken away, and your sin atoned for."

And I heard the voice of the Lord saying, "Whom shall I send, and who will go for us?" Then I said, "Here I am! Send me."

This encounter with God and experience of worship is not unique to Isaiah. In interacting with Isaiah, God is actually giving us an example for our own story. We are all Isaiah! And we all come to Him on His terms.

And so within these eight short verses, we see a gospel template of five primary liturgical movements.

MOVEMENT 1: CALL TO WORSHIP

God called Isaiah into His presence and revealed His glory to him! Isaiah probably didn't expect that this would happen, as this kind of theophany was rare, even for a prophet. Yet there God was, jarring

Isaiah out of his worship-as-usual routine with a life-changing opportunity to see Him high and lifted up.

Similarly, God has promised that He will meet with us when we gather in His name, and has even invited us to stand before the throne of His glorious presence through the blood of His Son, Jesus. Yet, like Isaiah, so many of us don't come to corporate worship expecting to see God move in any significant way. We need to be reminded that He is who He says He is, and He is inviting us to meet with Him!

And so the worship leader calls the congregation to worship in order to remind them to come as they are into the presence of the living God, placing all their wins, losses, brokenness, success, joy, and pain at the feet of Jesus. The leader is to remind worshipers, "No matter what is going on in the world or in your life, God is still on His throne and He is ever worthy of our worship."

MOVEMENT 2: ADORATION | PRAISE | THANKSGIVING

Upon coming into God's presence, Isaiah is overwhelmed by the angels' radical adoration and praise of God's holiness. In the same way, as God invites us into His presence, we immediately collide with His blatantly magnificent holiness. We see that He is unlike anything on this planet. He is completely holy. Completely gracious and compassionate. Completely slow to anger and abounding in lovingkindness. He is not like us, we are not like Him, and we cannot help but stand in awe and cry out in adoration, praise, and thanksgiving!

> The worship leader calls the congregation to come into the presence of the living God, placing all their wins, losses, brokenness, success, joy, and pain at the feet of Jesus.

The worship leader has the responsibility and privilege to use any and every tool at their disposal to show the congregation just how wonderful, amazing, and holy God is. To teach God-centered, doctrinally rich songs that remind people of who God is and what He has done, and magnify His greatness for everyone to see, hear, and sing. To read Scriptures that remind everyone how mighty and huge and wonderful and other-worldly He is! The worship leader is expanding people's views of their great God and inspiring them to reverently adore Him.

This is not fluff! This is foundational. As long as we see God as small, we will always see ourselves as bigger and more important than we really are. So we must endeavor to sing songs of adoration and praise and thanksgiving that show God's greatness.

MOVEMENT 3: CONFESSION | REPENTANCE

Upon seeing the ongoing adoration and praise of God's holiness, Isaiah was undone and cried out in confession that he was unclean. In the same way, when we come into God's presence, we become acutely aware of the stark contrast between our holiness (or lack there of) and God's. The Holy Spirit begins to shake the foundations of our souls and we are undone as we see how desperate we are for Him to come to us and cleanse us from all of our sin. Like Isaiah, we begin to confess our sins and repent to the Lord.

We need this time of confession and repentance in corporate worship, and the worship leader acts as the lead confessor and lead repenter. He is a catalyst, helping people come to God with all of their sin and shame over all of the ways they have failed their Creator by choosing to worship and trust in created things.

MOVEMENT 4: ASSURANCE

God is far too kind, far too loving of a Father to let Isaiah lie there wallowing in his sins. Without skipping a beat, He mercifully responds by sending an angel to touch a flaming coal to the prophet's lips and assure him that his sins have been atoned for.

Similarly, we have a wonderful promise that "if we confess our sins, he is faithful and just to forgive us our sins and cleanse us from all unrighteousness" (1 John 1:9). As we come to Him in repentance, the Lord picks us up and assures us that He has atoned for our sins, that our guilt is taken away, and that we are forgiven because of the work of Jesus Christ on the cross in our place, for our sins.

We need this time in the corporate worship service to remember our assurance in Christ alone. We rehearse this gospel truth to remind us that even our most noble works, intentions, and ideals could never save us. In fact, it is for those damnable "good works" that Jesus died.

The worship leader must remind the congregation that the cross was not just some event that happened two thousand years ago but has no impact on us now. Through songs, prayers, readings, and more, he or she leads the congregation in hopeful, joyful proclamation that because of Jesus' death and resurrection—and that work alone—we are not left in our sins. We have been forgiven and our guilt is taken away.

MOVEMENT 5: SENDING | COMMITMENT

Isaiah gets up off his face, now able to join in with the heavenly adoration, and within that context of praise, God immediately asks, "Whom shall I send, and who will go for us?" He has not only saved Isaiah from something, but to something, and in response to this overwhelming kindness, Isaiah wholeheartedly commits himself to carry out the mission of God in the world.

The same is true of us. God has not saved us from our sin so that we might live comfortable lives. He called us from death to life, and set us apart for works He prepared for us before the beginning of time; namely, to be living sacrifices who magnify the name and glory of Jesus in the world. He sends us into the world to be salt and light, a city on a hill that shines for His fame. And like Isaiah, we respond by shouting, "Here I am! Send me!" and committing to live a lifestyle of worship that is worthy of this great gospel He has entrusted us with.

People need time to be called to mission and commitment. The worship leader's songs, prayers, and readings must remind the people who have assembled that they have come to worship, not for the sake of feeling better about themselves, and that worship doesn't end when the services do. The worship of Jesus Christ and proclamation of His gospel are to extend into every area of their lives because all of life is worship.

As worship leaders, when we are planning for corporate worship, we are not planning a "set list." This is not a rock concert or a show. We are planning for maximum exposure to and engagement with truth of who God is, what He has done, and how that affects who we are and what we do in our families, neighborhoods, city, nation, and in all of creation.

Each movement of the liturgy plays a uniquely important role within the service, because each portion accomplishes a different gospel purpose and acts as an indispensable plotline in the grand narrative. The worship leader is a servant and representative of Christ, shepherding the people while telling this story in the best, fullest, most engaging way possible.

> The worship of Jesus Christ [is] to extend into every area of our lives because all of life is worship.

God has been incredibly kind to give us a plethora of tools with which to tell His story. There are thousands of psalms, hymns, and spiritual songs, both ancient and modern, that effectively communicate and engage with each plotline. In most churches the songs tend to dominate the liturgy, and for a very good reason. However, one should never feel constrained to just be a song leader.

God has given us His Word, and while each song should be saturated with the truth of the Bible, we should never shy away from reading the Scriptures in corporate worship. Jonathan Edwards spoke of the Bible, saying, "Be assiduous in reading the Holy Scriptures. This is the fountain whence all knowledge in divinity must be derived. Therefore let not this treasure lie by you neglected." He knew the value of Scripture, and we would do well to learn from him. It is impossible to improve on God's Word. It's impossible to have too much Bible in our services. Our times together should be drenched in it and dripping with the condensation of its truth.

While most corporate worship songs are prayers in themselves, we have a remarkable opportunity to worship and teach through spoken prayers as well. On multiple occasions, Jesus taught His disciples through spoken prayers. As we pray thoughtfully and pastorally, we are giving an example of prayer for people to use in their daily lives as well.

Finally, spoken encouragement can also be an incredibly helpful tool to use as you seek to serve and lead a congregation in a holistic expression of worship. Jesus refers to those in His church as His sheep, and for good reason. People need to be taught not only by example but by exhortation as well. Giving verbal instructions

> It's impossible to have too much Bible in our services. Our times together should be drenched in it.

as to why we sing, raise our hands, or kneel, for instance, is an excellent way to lead people who are looking for permission to express their praise and adoration to God—or perhaps simply need to be jarred out of their routine and reminded of God's goodness and love.

As we step onto the platform, we are telling the story of God to the people we are leading. By the power of the Holy Spirit, that story will inevitably shape them as worshipers. The question will be, "What and who are they worshiping?" Will it be the story of a great God who has rescued us from our sins and His wrath by Himself and for Himself? The great God who has called us into His presence to worship Him in the splendor of His holiness? The Holy One who has called us to a great mission for His name and glory?

This story is too magnificent, too perfect to neglect! It's the kind of story that every storyteller dreams of being able to tell, and so we must strive to become master storytellers if we would do it justice! Otherwise, like the kids left wondering what happened to the puppy and the pigeon, many unfamiliar with the gospel may be left wondering about the blessed hope of the Cross.

QUESTIONS FOR LEADERS

1. What hesitations would you have to changing the structure of your service to a more formal or historic liturgy?

2. What songs do you have in your corporate worship music repertoire that most effectively communicate the story of the gospel individually? How can you order those to tell the story most effectively and collectively in a service?

3. How often in a typical worship service do you include hymns or worship songs that either quote or reference Bible truths about the gospel or God's redemptive plan through Jesus, His Son?

WORSHIP LEADERS

7

WE ARE
EVANGELISTS

I cannot think of a more appropriate Scripture passage for worship leaders than the first five verses of 2 Timothy 4. Though not explicitly written to worship leaders, the passage is a perfect encouragement for those whose responsibility and privilege it is to take the platform each week to lead God's church in corporate worship.

While Paul is training this young leader to pastor well, we do well to learn from his teaching:

> *I charge you in the presence of God and of Christ Jesus,*
> *who is to judge the living and the dead, and by his*
> *appearing and his kingdom: preach the word; be ready in*
> *season and out of season; reprove, rebuke, and exhort,*

with complete patience and teaching. For the time is
coming when people will not endure sound teaching, but
having itching ears they will accumulate for themselves
teachers to suit their own passions, and will turn away
from listening to the truth and wander off into myths. As
for you, always be sober-minded, endure suffering, do the
work of an evangelist, fulfill your ministry (vv. 1–5).

Paul is both serious and realistic as he warns us not to fall for the seductive lies of the world and be carried away by its mythical ear-tickling passions. How powerful the cultural current that wants dulled-down, comfortable worship; how great the gravitational pull of the world.

Yet we can confidently fulfill our ministry knowing that greater still is the irresistible pull of the Holy Spirit as He draws men to the gospel of grace. This great gospel helps us to be sober-minded as we endure the suffering we will receive from patiently preaching and teaching the Word.

Paul seems to sum up our ministry as worship leaders by calling each of us an "evangelist." The term "evangelist" is used sparingly in the New Testament, and it is completely absent from the Old.

Over the years, the Lord has blessed me to know and serve alongside several men who legitimately have the gift of evangelism, and I am incredibly grateful for them.

Yet for the longest time, when I heard the word "evangelist," I often felt like I was being taken back in a time machine to my childhood, when our churches would have weeklong "revivals." Our church leaders would always bring in various traveling evangelists who would tell beyond-belief stories and try to force as many on-the-spot decisions as possible. Our youth group would often attend weekend retreats, summer camps, and evangelism conferences that would feature many of these same speakers.

One rather vivid memory from a particular week at camp stands out above the others

I can see myself staring at a picture of a little girl on the screen. The evangelist says: "Look at this picture. Look at this little girl. Little Lucy left the revival last week and didn't accept Jesus. On the way home she got in a car wreck and died and went to hell. You don't wanna go to hell, do you? If you leave here and get in a car wreck, you're gonna go to hell. Don't let that happen. Everyone bow your head and close your eyes.... No one looking around."

And everyone bows their heads.

"I'm gonna count to three and snap my fingers and when I do I want you to raise your hand.

"One ... two. Don't let me get to three, just raise that hand right now—yes, I see that hand.... I see that hand.... Thank you."

Music continues to play softly in the background. And then the evangelist says earnestly once more, "Don't let this moment pass you by ..."

"One ... two ... three.... Raise your hands!"

He snaps his fingers and hundreds of hands go up. They all crowd the stage, and he leads them to pray a magical prayer that will come in handy as a "Get Out of Hell Free" card someday.

Certainly hell is real and I don't want anyone to go there. Jesus talked about hell a lot in order to warn us of the consequences of our sins. He didn't paint it to be a place that anyone would ever want to go.

But to me this guy felt more like he was using manipulative scare tactics. This was more of a commercial against hell than a message of hope that we can be saved from our sins and live in fellowship with Jesus forever.

And then there were the televangelists I grew up watching on TV. You know, the guys who pass out nice little spiritual anecdotes and then ask for your money but later get busted for money laundering and do time in jail—those guys.

My dad made these guys a running joke around my house growing up. He had bought a VHS tape that spotlighted a well-known televangelist all decked out in his suit, asking people for money in exchange for miracles. With every third word, it seemed, he would close his eyes really tightly and shake his head and you would hear an overdubbed farting noise. Then he would say something silly like, "I feel the power of the Lord's anointing coming out of me right now!" This kind of crude little-boy humor made our whole family literally roll on the floor laughing.

For the longest time those were the images conjured up in my mind when I hear the word "evangelist." The word sounded icky—like I've just been drenched with a bucket of the green slime from an old Nickelodeon game show.

Now I can say that I am very grateful to know personally that all evangelists aren't this way. Over the years, I have worked with many who have given their entire lives to make much of Jesus by proclaiming the gospel to those who have never heard it before. I have nothing but the utmost respect for them. When I'm around them, I want to love Jesus more. They are fresh with the aroma of heaven. They have a zeal to make the name of Jesus known and an anointing in the way they share the gospel with people. They live by faith and display an inspiring confidence in the Holy Spirit's redemptive power. At the same time, they maintain an appropriate understanding of their own responsibility to preach the gospel and give people every opportunity to respond.

For such godly men I have a deep admiration, and it's easy for me to look at them and say, "I wish I had the gift of evangelism like that."

The word *evangelist* literally means a

> The word *evangelist* literally means a zealous advocate for something or someone.

zealous advocate for something or someone. So I could be an evangelist for anything and my particular personality makes me really good at it.

If I love a movie, I want to tell everyone I know about it. If there is a particularly good restaurant that I come across, I want to broadcast it to the world.

For example, a few nights ago I took my wife on a date to try a new restaurant in St. Louis. We had heard good things about this particular restaurant and wanted to give it a shot. As a native Texan, I enjoy few things as much as great Tex-Mex food. When you're in Texas, great Tex-Mex restaurants are everywhere you turn. Even the bad Tex-Mex restaurants are still good. This can be somewhat problematic if you're trying to watch your weight.

But when we moved to St. Louis, it quickly became apparent to us that good Tex-Mex did not exist in the Midwest. Finally, after almost three years into living here we found it. There we sat, enjoying some of the best food we had tasted since moving.

What did we do? We pulled out our phones and texted all of our friends that they had to try this place. We started planning double dates with other couples because we wanted to share the enjoyment of the experience with them.

We are all that way to some extent. In sharing our enjoyment, our enjoyment somehow becomes even more fulfilling! Think about your Facebook, Twitter, Pinterest, and Instagram feeds. Your friends are all evangelists for the things they love.

And you are too. A great cup of coffee. A culinary masterpiece. A good cause. A presidential candidate. You want to spread the good news.

But specifically as worship leaders, we are evangelists who zealously proclaim the

> As worship leaders, we are evangelists who zealously proclaim the best news of all . . . the good news of Jesus Christ.

best news of all, the message of the gospel (which literally means "good news"). There is no message more worthy of the time we spend together in corporate worship than the good news of Jesus Christ. There is no message more powerful and none more fitting to be gathered around to sing about and pray in thanksgiving.

As evangelists, worship leaders should not be ashamed of the gospel, but proclaim it with all the passion we possibly can, knowing that it is the death-abolishing, eternal life-giving power of God for salvation to all who believe! It can heal every spiritual affliction and strengthen us with faith, without which it's impossible to please God (Romans 16:25–27 Hebrews 11:6).

Of course, the very word *gospel* has been hijacked by many to be a buzzword that means whatever we want it to mean.

Gospel music. Gospel brunch. Gospel beard. There's also gospel-centered. Gospel-driven. And even (ugh!) gospeliscious.

"He really gospeled me as we were gospeling each other."

It can get confusing, especially if you grew up in the church. What is the gospel *actually*?

This is the gospel (with some important background to help us understand why it is such good news):

→ That God, the infinitely holy, merciful, just, loving, sovereign King over all, created all things good. That mankind sinned and was subjected along with all of creation to the consequences of sin; namely, death, suffering, sickness, and brokenness.

→ That before the creation of the world, God knew we would sin, but lovingly chose to create us anyway so that He could redeem and adopt us for the glory of His name.

→ That at just the right time God sent His Son, Jesus, to be born to a virgin, live a perfect life, and die a perfect death in our place for our sins.

→ That Jesus' blood alone can wash us clean and make us holy. His work alone can save us. His salvation is by grace alone, that we receive by faith—a salvation that is His free and completely undeserved gift to us. We could not earn it with all the trying in the world.

→ That Jesus has promised to come again to defeat sin, death, and suffering once and for all. That He will make all things new and restore everything to its indescribable former glory. He will reign forever, and we will worship Him for all of eternity with an unending delight because we will know Him fully as we are fully known.

That is the gospel story. And note that we are not the heroes of this story. Jesus is!

That's what makes this a message of hope. That's what makes this good news. It will not disappoint because God Himself has promised our spiritual salvation, and He Himself will carry it through.

This gospel is the greatest story in the world and it's true.

This ought to infect every area of our lives! It should be what we talk about with our families, our friends, and our neighbors. It should be the topic of discussion around the dinner table and the pool table, at the community block parties and the childrens' birthday parties—and certainly in our corporate worship services.

> We are not the heroes of this gospel story. Jesus is! This gospel is the greatest story in the world and it's *true*.

As worship leaders, we are positioned to do the work of evangelists in a unique way—to be messengers who tell the good news as zealously and passionately as we can, using one of the most naturally passionate mediums in existence.

As we lead the church of God in singing the truth of God, He has promised to use the truth to set people free.

At Pentecost in Acts 2, we see God the Holy Spirit coming to fill His church with power. In a miraculous Babel-in-reverse-type display, the Spirit enables God's people to declare the gospel to men from every nation and language in a way that they could all understand. Where at Babel He had confused their languages, here He was at work uniting their languages.

While we don't know exactly what they were saying, we do know that they were praising God and declaring His mighty works. This display of praise left people amazed and perplexed. And this multicultural, multi-language display not only prepared the hearers for Peter's clear and pointed preaching of the gospel but acted in concert with the preached Word.

The result? Three thousand people were saved.

The sung Word of God is naturally designed to be just as evangelistic as the preached Word of God. When the church is singing to God and praising Him for who He is and what He has done, we are corporately acting as a major, positive announcement for His goodness, faithfulness, righteousness, holiness, and excellence. We are using one of the world's most powerful mediums to truthfully tell each other and everyone

> The privilege has been given to us to work hard as evangelists so that our churches speak the truth of God in the most effective, affection-filled way possible.

who is listening that God is superior to all other things. Talk about truth in advertising.

So the responsibility falls to us to not be lazy in the way we proclaim God's message. The privilege has been given to us to work hard as evangelists and be very selective in the songs that we sing, ensuring that each word we put in the mouths of our churches speaks the truth of God in the most effective, affection-filled way possible. We must strive to be creatively, compellingly, and artfully engaging as we present the greatest message on Earth.

As we do this, we can be confident that God has guaranteed that He will have His way with His Word and it will not return empty. As we sow the seed and water the seed, we can trust God to be faithful to His promise to make the seed grow and produce fruit (Isaiah 55:10–11)—a miracle none of us could take credit for.

Each week, as we do the work of evangelists and declare the Word of God in our songs, prayers, Scripture readings, calls to worship, benedictions, and more, God is giving new life to men and women even as they hear and sing along. He is using the preached and sung Word, removing hearts of stone, and giving them new hearts of flesh that can respond to the irresistible wooing of the Holy Spirit. Because He is doing the work, we are not laboring in vain. We are laboring that the greatest message on earth would be heard, that all may taste and see that the Lord is good, and that hearts would turn to the all-satisfying love and all-sufficient work of Christ. What a joy. What a privilege.

QUESTIONS FOR LEADERS

1. In what ways have you, as a worship leader, felt society's pressure to present a "dulled-down, comfortable worship"? Have you ever succumbed to that cultural pressure in choosing (or not choosing) certain music?

2. Do you have any hesitations about evangelism? What are they? How will you overcome that?

3. Do you believe God can use your leadership and songs to save people? Do you believe He wants to?

WORSHIP | LEADERS

ARTISTS

Each morning I stumble out of bed, brush my teeth, and walk upstairs to get my four children ready for school. It is difficult for a guy like me to imagine that anything good can happen in the world before 8 a.m. Coffee cannot be finished brewing early enough at that time of day.

This morning is particularly difficult to get up. It is winter in St. Louis and even the thermometer itself seems to be shivering as it boasts a frigid temperature of 27 degrees. On mornings like this, nothing feels better than staying in bed under a warm blanket. I am not excited about getting up. But I somehow manage it.

As I get my kids ready, we realize they need to clean out their backpacks, because the packs have grown to be stuffed to the max with anything and everything you could imagine. Papers, toys, old food . . . I might have been convinced one of them was hiding Jimmy Hoffa's body in there, if I thought any of them actually knew who he was.

As they each empty their bags, they begin to show off for me their various projects they've been working on in school. My four-year-old son hands me a painting of a rainbow, vibrant and bright with every color you can imagine. Certainly not consistent with the ROYGBIV spectrum, but when you're a kid, who cares?

As I make a big deal about how great his painting is, my nine-year-old daughter marches right over to the refrigerator and proudly hangs a very well-done drawing of our family. With surprising detail, she draws my raven black hair and chiseled physique as well as my wife's beautiful blonde hair and smile that could rival any sunset. She got her brothers' curly hair and mohawk just right. She even gets the cat's black fur, white paws, and green eyes. It is quite impressive.

All of my children love to write and act and sing and dance and draw and paint—just like their dad. And seeing my kids creating and loving art the way I do moves my heart. It makes their dad proud.

I can't help but think that this is how God feels when His children, who He created in His image, reflect His creative genius.

Genesis 1–2 paints a beautiful picture of a creative God imagining and inventing and investing His creative purpose into a beautiful, perfect, and good world that He delights in. With excitement He spoke the heavens and the earth into being. He made the sun and then artfully scattered its light rays across the sky to create a beautiful sunrise like nothing we could imagine. Then He did it again in the evening to make a breathtaking sunset before breathing the moon and stars into being to light the night.

God thought up the highest mountain and the deepest canyon. He made rivers and lakes and oceans and trillions of grains of sand to cover both their beaches and the deserts that would never see them. He made giant blue whales and tiny goldfish, majestic lions and cute kittens. Then monkeys and mackerels, moose and mice, mules and moles, mammoths and mallards, mustangs and marsupials.

He was thorough. He was having fun. He was painting pictures with His imagination and then bringing them to life with the power of His words!

Then He came to the sixth day and created something that had been in His heart since long before that first day. From eternity past, He had in mind to create man and woman in His image. Not because He needed us, but because He wanted us. Not because He was lacking anything or felt some sort of lonely void, but because He wanted to give of His overflowing, overabundant glory.

He wanted to graciously share the infinite beauty of His glory and holiness, and so He created everything with much excitement and great pleasure, as He exclaimed, "Very good!"

G. K. Chesterton says in his book *Orthodoxy*:

> *The sun rises every morning ... it might be true that the sun rises regularly because He never gets tired of rising. His routine might be due, not to a lifelessness, but to a rush of life.*

God made oceans and trillions of grains of sand to cover both their beaches and the deserts. He made giant blue whales and tiny goldfish, majestic lions and cute kittens.

The thing I mean can be seen, for instance, in children, when they find some game or joke that they specially enjoy. A child kicks his legs rhythmically through excess, not absence, of life. Because children have abounding vitality, because they are in spirit fierce and free, therefore they want things repeated and unchanged. They always say, "Do it again"; and the grown-up person does it again until he is nearly dead....

It is possible that God says every morning, "Do it again" to the sun; and every evening, "Do it again" to the moon. It may not be automatic necessity that makes all daisies alike; it may be that God makes every daisy separately, but has never got tired of making them. It may be that He has the eternal appetite of infancy; for we have sinned and grown old, and our Father is younger than we.[1]

Pablo Picasso profoundly echoed Chesterton's sentiment by stating, "Every child is an artist. The problem is how to remain an artist once we grow up."

I dare say he did not mean "How do we remain copycats?" Or "How do we continue to learn the systems, processes, and sciences of art well enough to make lots of money, fame, and success out of it as a career?"

Certainly there is an innate desire to be delighted in every child who sits at a table painting rainbows on a white paper canvas. Children create not only because it makes them happy, but also to make others happy. There is an optimistic innocence that says, "I get to create something people will enjoy," that is untainted by worldly ulterior motives of the renown that they might gain from it. Children aren't sitting there daydreaming of all the financial implications of making it big.

When my six-year-old daughter prances downstairs all dolled up in her dress-up shoes, clothes, earrings, and makeup, having just choreographed a new dance and exuberantly proclaims, "Daddy! Look at me!" it never crosses my mind to question her motives. She is having fun and wants her dad to delight in her. And I do.

In the same way, the Lord has created us in His image to be creative as He is creative. He made us for song and dance, for finger painting and watercolors and murals to beautify the world. To write sonnets and symphonies, epics and études. He fashioned us with palates and imaginations and gave us access to herbs and spices so that we could come up with some of the greatest culinary masterpieces the world has ever known.

The Artist made us artists. And all so that we might reflect the beauty of His character and the wonder of His story! The art we are blessed to create is all ultimately intended to point to the Creator.

Of course there are art forms that are more naturally engineered to explicitly explain the glorious gospel message more effectively than others. For example, I may not naturally draw a line from a mouth watering, exquisite plate of veal medallions in raspberry truffle sauce to the redemptive work of Christ on the cross. And though I may be moved to tears by the beauty of a painting, I may or may not immediately come to the correct interpretation of what message it is attempting to convey.

> The Artist made us artists so that we might reflect the beauty of His character and the wonder of His story.

The arts are often abstract and mysterious, echoes of the mystery surrounding an infinite God—billows of smoke rising from the raging fire of His holiness. First Corinthians 13:12 tells us that because of the fall, even on our best day we can only see a poor reflection of Him, like we are looking at a circus mirror. His holiness is too great for our finite eyes and minds.

And yet we have the mind of Christ (1 Corinthians 2:16), which means we can know Him because of Christ's redemptive work on our behalf. We can strive to create art that brings clarity to the mystery. That makes the abstract apparent. That hears past the echo, straight to its source. That looks past the smoke, straight into the fire.

As worship leaders, this is what we strive for. We are artists—curators and creators of art that makes the mystery more comprehensible. We diligently work to put on display the Invisible with the most beautiful mediums we can.

But for the worship leader, the medium is not our message—*it is the vehicle for our message*.

In the church, art is a wonderful servant but a terrible master. While we strive to use art to communicate the glory of God, the art is always subservient to its intended purpose; namely, making Jesus famous—to glorify and honor Him in the sight of all who hear and see.

I dare not denigrate any worship leader who is diligently seeking to put the glory of God on display, but it is incredibly easy for us to get the cart before the horse and begin to "do art for art's sake." As this begins to happen, our services grow more and more difficult to engage with.

> The arts are often abstract and mysterious, echoes of the mystery surrounding an infinite God. Even on our best day we can only see a poor reflection of Him.

This may look drastically different depending on the personality of the worship leaders and the contexts we are leading in.

For the high-production, technically driven worship leaders, our songs can almost effortlessly become unsingable. In the name of creativity, we gravitate toward copious amounts of vocal ornamentation and performance-driven pop songs in keys that few can sing along with.

For the hipster worship leaders who are cynical of the overproduced, popular Christian subculture, we run in the exact opposite direction, and our services can easily become overrun by unmemorable shoe-gazer music that is equally difficult to sing along with.

The God-given creativity we want so badly to use to help people connect with God actually ends up alienating the people we are attempting to lead from being able to engage.

I could give examples of this in high church, low church, attractional church, missional church, seeker church, cowboy church, biker church, and more.

But no matter which scenario we naturally gravitate toward, in the church, art for art's sake always draws the most attention to itself and creates a spectator environment. And so people think they can stand back and let the professionals handle all of the heavy lifting.

This is certainly not what we want when we are seeking to help people rehearse the gospel together. We want to make it as easy as possible for people to engage as we call them to make melody with their hearts to the Lord. Worship leaders want to help God's people encourage one another with psalms, hymns, and spiritual songs in corporate worship.

We are leading a kingdom of priests whom the Lord has redeemed and given access through Jesus to the splendor of His presence, that we might all stand together unified as one body and worship Him with one voice. This is a family activity. And a good worship leader creates great art that effectively engages the whole family in worship.

I say *great* art intentionally. Labeling something Christian does not give it a pass to stink. In fact, it should be the exact opposite. Anything that bears the name of Christ ought to be the best thing in the world.

And why not? We are created in the image of the ultimate Creative Genius, who now lives inside all who believe upon the name of Jesus Christ!

What greater source of inspiration could we have than the One who paints the skies and rejoices over us with singing? What greater tutor and mentor could we have than the One who invented invention, innovated innovation, imagined imagination, and created creativity?

Yet too often the church produces mediocre-at-best art, puts a Christian label on it, and calls it quits. We fail to be thoughtfully innovative and instead settle for being a copy of a copy of a copy of something that was introduced in the mainstream years earlier. This pattern of behavior over the last few decades has caused Christian music to become infamous for its laziness.

I have heard the saying, "Those who can, do. Those who can't, teach." This is degrading, and as the son of two teachers I can testify that this is certainly not true.

But sadly, a similar saying exists that goes, "Those who can, do. Those who can't, make Christian music instead."

How is it that we have allowed this to happen? Have we already gotten old? Did we grow calloused to the wonder and excitement of God's glory? Did we lose the joy of delighting our Father with the art we get the privilege of creating?

> We all are to stand unified and worship Him with one voice. A good worship leader creates great art that effectively engages the whole family in worship.

Was it for the money, for the bottom line? Did we exchange the glory of the Creator who is blessed forever for the almighty dollar?

Have we forgotten who we are? Have we forgotten who our Father is?

Worship leaders, we must aim to make the greatest art that we possibly can to serve the greatest purpose that we were created for. We must labor to weave words together into a musical tapestry that makes much of the only One worthy of being made much of.

We must fight the pride that would infect and distort our holy creativity and cause us to seek to lift ourselves up in the place of our Master.

Art is work. There is a reason God modeled for us to rest on the seventh day. He never halfway did anything. He never made junk. He never made anything He was ashamed of. Everything He made was perfect. It was either good or very good. It was satisfying. It was fun. And though He was having fun, delighting in His imagination and inventing thing after thing that revealed Himself to us, He rested at the end of it all.

Was He tired? Winded? Never! The Lord doesn't grow weary. But His example of resting reminds mortal men that creativity is hard work. It is work worth doing—and doing well.

Because of His creative work, we can know Him. Romans 1:18-20 tells us that the beauty He has made has left us without any excuses. He has revealed Himself to us through creation, and through His Son, Jesus, He has given us the privilege to do the same.

Worship leaders, we are artists who have been given these talents so that we

> Labor to weave words together into a musical tapestry that makes much of the only One worthy of being made much of.

might bring a return to our Master, that we might make Him known. We have been given the gifts of art and song and creativity so that we might, in new, beautiful, and inventive ways, display the supremacy of God to the watching world through the church. He has given us these powerful mediums to carry a powerful message.

So let us carry the message high and carry it proud, with breathtaking songs and epic stories, masterful paintings and majestic poetry. Worship leaders, let us carry the message well.

As we do, just as I delight in my daughter's refrigerator art, I believe our Father will delight in us as we reflect His heart.

QUESTIONS FOR LEADERS

1. How much time do you spend each week on creativity?

2. "Art is a wonderful servant, but a terrible master." In what ways can artistic elements in the worship service threaten to overwhelm the purpose of worship—to bring glory to Jesus Christ? Has this ever happened in your church? If so, explain what occurred.

3. What creative elements have you or members of your worship team considered in the past? Were any adopted? If so, how did they work?

4. How do you define excellence in art and music? Do you believe that excellence is somehow less spiritual? If so, why? Is that biblical?

WORSHIP LEADERS

WE ARE
CHRISTIANS

Each week we spend 168 hours of living in the world. Most Christians spend around one hour of that in corporate worship. So to say that our corporate worship is the sum of Christian worship is kinda silly. It's like saying, "God, here is 1/168th of my life. I'll keep the rest."

Certainly songs and sermons are key elements in the Christian life. As pastors and ministers, we have invested years in crafting church services so they draw worshipers closer to God.

But I would argue that as powerful and helpful as they are, church services are potentially our smallest expressions of worship. Being a Christian is about so much more than going to a church building on the weekends.

Everywhere we go, we are living representatives of the living God. Every place we go is His.

The mall is God's.

The fast lane . . . God's.

The computer late at night . . . God's.

The coffee shop where you meet your friends . . . God's.

The dinner table with your family during the holidays . . . God's.

It all belongs to Him. It's all by Him, through Him, and to Him. And who He is demands our worship in every arena of our lives.

The apostle Paul tells us in 1 Corinthians 6:19–20 that we are not our own, but are bought with a price and should honor God with our bodies because they are temples that carry the presence of God.

He goes on to explain what that kind of honoring God looks like in 1 Corinthians 10:31, writing, "Whether you eat or drink, or whatever you do, do it all to the glory of God."

"Whatever you do . . ." This leaves no exceptions. It means everything you do. That your entire life is being offered back up to God as an offering of worship. That you are, as Romans 12 tells us, "a living sacrifice."

Missiologists Michael Frost and Alan Hirsch describe this all-encompassing kind of worship in their book *ReJesus*, writing,

> *Worship as the Bible characterizes it cannot be limited to singing praise and worship songs to God. Although it includes this, it is far more all-encompassing than that. Worship is nothing less than **offering our whole lives back to God though Jesus.** It is taking all the elements that make up human life (family, friendships, money, work, nation, etc.) and presenting them back to the One who gives them their ultimate meaning in the first place.*[1]

If worship is truly offering our entire world back to God, then worship leaders are leading the church in worship in a much more extreme and radical way than just standing on a stage and singing songs. We are showing them what it means to be a Christian.

In every area of our lives, we are to be examples of people who live in the obedience of faith in Christ (Romans 1:5) and help others do the same.

So while we have looked in detail at worship leaders as pastors and teachers and artists and evangelists and even storytellers on a stage, I would hate for you to get the idea that you're off the hook from doing these things out in the real world. That somehow being an evangelist from the stage gives you a pass from sharing the gospel with your friends. That being a pastor on the weekends means you are exempt from the Great Commission to make disciples. That we are somehow more than normal Christians.

As worship leaders, we often view ourselves as exceptions to the rule when it comes to these things that we desire for and even expect from our people as hallmarks of a believer. That somehow being in vocational ministry puts us in a different category.

Perhaps more than the average person, we tend to think about worship—all of its nuances and applications—for the people we are leading. But because of the nature of our vocation, we miss the forest for the trees, making worship primarily about the corporate experience. We end up dwelling on how to create effective and excellent corporate worship services.

Rather than worship ministry drawing us nearer to God in our personal lives, we use it as a license to drift from Him, to disobey Him.

We say we should be people who read our Bibles, and we ask God from the stage

> We often read the Bible only to get more material for the coming weekend, rather than to know God and think rightly about Him.

to show us who He is through His Word. But in practice we often read the Bible only to check it off the list or to get more material for the coming weekend, rather than to know God and think rightly about Him so that we might draw near to Him in worship each day.

We say we should be people of prayer and we spend time each week preparing eloquent prayers for the platform. Yet we struggle when it comes to actually talking to God in private.

In our services, we pray corporately that God would send us out into the world to be the church who makes disciples, telling people the good news of what Christ has done for them. But in practice we are often so busy "doing ministry" that we miss out on the everyday opportunities to share Christ with our friends, families, and neighbors.

We say we exist to make the name and glory of Jesus famous, but in practice much of our time is spent exhausting our efforts to make our own name and glory famous. Many times we are not seeking to tell and retell the story of Jesus. We are seeking to write our own story where we are the heroes.

And that's what it boils down to in the end. We love our names. We love our glory. We love our fame.

We want to be rock stars.

That's why rock star worship syndrome has nothing to do with church models, musical styles, or fashion sense. It has everything to do with our hearts.

We don't need a redefining of worship leadership as much as we need a reawakening to how great Jesus is.

He cannot be contained. He cannot be squeezed in. He is infinite. He is a fire that consumes all He touches.

He is the sun around which everything

> We don't need
> a redefining
> of worship
> leadership [but]
> a reawakening
> to how great
> Jesus is.

revolves—the light that will shine into eternity and give light to everyone. His is the name that the saints and the angels will be shouting forever. It's certainly not ours!

As the hymn proclaims, "His praise and glory shall not fail through all eternity!" The same cannot be said of us.

He is not like us. His ways are higher than ours. Hypothetically speaking, if there were any foolishness in Him, it would still be wiser than our wisest day. If there were any weakness in Him, it would still be stronger than our strongest day.

His glory is unparalleled. His beauty is unmatched. His holiness uncompromised. He has no rival!

That kind of incomparable glory humbles us and puts us in our rightful place because it reminds us that He is exalted in His rightful place—on His throne, sovereign over all.

He has purchased us out of death and darkness. The King over all creation has redeemed us, adopted us, and called us his own. We are not our own. We are His!

He is for us. He is with us. Forever.

That is enough for us. That is our affirmation. That is our motivation.

That is the reason that we repent of grasping at the straws of our own esteem and refuse to believe the lie that we are somehow above normal Christianity.

That is the reason that we strive to be pastors, theologians, and evangelists not just on a stage but even more out in the world we live in. It is the reason we cannot be so caught up in ministry that we miss God and what He is doing in everyday life.

This begins not by asking the question, "How do I lead our church well?" Or, "How can I expand my influence?" Not by devising strategies or working harder.

This begins by slowing down and asking, "Who is God? Who does He say I am? What does His Word say He desires from my life? Where is He at work right now? How is the Holy Spirit leading me? What is He asking of me?"

And then *actually doing* what He says.

This is everyday, normal Christianity. This is run of the mill. There is nothing rock star about it. This will not earn us esteem. It will not achieve for us status in the inner circle of influential movements.

It will not give us chart-topping worship records or opportunities to sign autographs. It may not make the people of our churches love us more or respond more to our leadership.

In fact, we may never see the effects of living a lifestyle of worship this side of eternity. But the King who is sovereign over all sees, and it makes Him happy. The only one worthy of your life sees, and it makes Him smile.

He isn't fickle. You don't have to earn His approval. You can't change His mind about you. He has already made up His mind to hide you in Christ and love you beyond all fairness and sanity.

We are His sons and daughters. We have an eternal inheritance— privileges we could have never dreamed of. We aren't beggars or paupers just trying to get a handout of approval from fickle people. We have more in Christ than we could imagine and certainly more than we could keep for ourselves.

That kind of abundant generosity nec-essarily flows out of the life of believers in all they say and do. It cannot be ignored. It seeps into the deepest, darkest places of our hearts and gives us new meaning, new significance.

> Our ministry begins by slowing down and asking, "Who is God? . . . What is He asking of me?" And then *actually doing* what He says.

Worship leaders, none of us is above that. None of us is exempt. None of us gets a pass from experiencing that kind of life change—a change that will make us conduits for God to bring that kind of grace into the world.

Let's slow down. Take a breath of fresh air. Enjoy the beauty of God's creation. Listen for His voice. Respond in obedience.

Let's stop trying so hard to be rock stars.

Let's be Christians.

NOTES

INTRODUCTION: ROCK STAR WORSHIP SYNDROME

1. Jonathan Edwards, "Some Thoughts Concerning the Revival," in *The Works of Jonathan Edwards*, vol. 4, 'The Great Awakening', ed. C. C. Goen (New Haven, CT: Yale Univ. Press, 1972), 387.

CHAPTER 3: WE ARE REDEEMED & ADOPTED

1. J. I. Packer, *Knowing God* (Downers Grove, IL: InterVarsity, 1973), 206.

CHAPTER 4: WE ARE DEACONS & PASTORS

1. J. Oswald Sanders, *Spiritual Leadership* (Chicago: Moody, 2007), chapter 6.

CHAPTER 5: WE ARE THEOLOGIANS

1. "Christian Knowledge," *The Works of Jonathan Edwards*, vol. 2, ed. Edward Hickman (Edinburgh: Banner of Truth, 1974), 162, as quoted in John Piper, *God's Passion for His Glory* (Wheaton, IL: Crossway, 1998), 35.

CHAPTER 8: WE ARE ARTISTS

1. G. K. Chesterton, *Orthodoxy* (San Francisco: Ignatius Press, 1995), 65–66.

CHAPTER 9: WE ARE CHRISTIANS

1. Michael Frost and Alan Hirsch, *ReJesus: A Wild Messiah for a Missional Church* (Peabody, MA: Hendrickson, 2009), 125. Boldface appears in the original.

GOSPEL JUSTICE

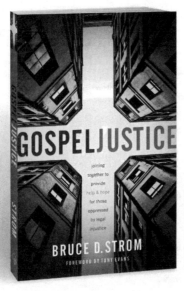

Bruce Strom left a successful legal career to start Administer Justice, a nonprofit ministry that provides free legal care to those in need in the name of Jesus through partnership with local churches. Now Strom is calling the church at large to take up the cause of justice. Through stories and principles this book shows the reader how he or she can be part of this movement and can participate in the cause of legal justice for the poor. It is an ideal resource for church leaders, Christian lawyers, businesspeople, and entrepreneurs.

Also available as an ebook

www.MoodyPublishers.com | GJI.org

HOW TO
WORSHIP JESUS CHRIST

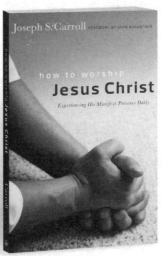

978-0-8024-0990-4

Can an ordinary person enter the presence of Christ or is that something that only happened for biblical characters? Maybe that question leads you to ask "What does it even mean to be in Jesus' presence?" In *How to Worship Jesus Christ*, Joseph Carroll explains what it means to enter Christ's presence and that it is something available to every Christian — through true worship.

Also available as an ebook

MOODY
PUBLISHERS

www.MoodyPublishers.com